CAMBRIDGE
Global English
Activity Book

Jane Boylan and Claire Medwell

CAMBRIDGE
UNIVERSITY PRESS

CAMBRIDGE
UNIVERSITY PRESS

University Printing House, Cambridge CB2 8BS, United Kingdom

Cambridge University Press is part of the University of Cambridge.

It furthers the University's mission by disseminating knowledge in the pursuit of education, learning and research at the highest international levels of excellence.

Information on this title: education.cambridge.org

© Cambridge University Press 2014

This publication is in copyright. Subject to statutory exception and to the provisions of relevant collective licensing agreements, no reproduction of any part may take place without the written permission of Cambridge University Press.

First published 2014
10th printing 2016

Printed in India by Multivista Global Pvt Ltd

A catalogue record for this publication is available from the British Library

ISBN 978-1-107-62123-7 Paperback

Cambridge University Press has no responsibility for the persistence or accuracy of URLs for external or third-party internet websites referred to in this publication, and does not guarantee that any content on such websites is, or will remain, accurate or appropriate.

CD 1	
Learner's Book	
Track number on CD	Track number in book
1	1
2	2
3	3
4	4
5	5
6	6
7	7
8	8
9	9
10	10
11	11
12	12
13	13
14	14
15	15
16	16
17	17
18	18
19	19
20	20
21	21
22	22
23	23
24	24
25	25
26	26
27	27
28	28
29	29
30	30
31	31

CD 2					
Learner's Book					
Track number on CD	Track number in book	Track number on CD	Track number in book	Track number on CD	Track number in book
1	32			**Activity Book**	
2	33			25	56
3	34			26	57
4	35			27	58
5	36			28	59
6	37			29	60
7	38			30	61
8	39			31	62
9	40			32	63
10	41			33	64
11	42			34	65
12	43			35	66
13	44			36	67
14	45			37	68
15	46			38	69
16	47			39	70
17	48				
18	49				
19	50				
20	51				
21	52				
22	53				
23	54				
24	55				

Contents

UNIT 1 Talking about people
1	Describing people	4
2	Our profiles	6
3	An interview	8
4	Favourite things	10
5	My favourite people	12
6	Unit 1 Revision	14
	My global progress	15

UNIT 2 Staying healthy
1	Common illnesses	16
2	Fever	18
3	Food and health	20
4	Health blogs	22
5	*Stone soup*	24
6	Unit 2 Revision	26
	My global progress	27

UNIT 3 Where we live
1	Describing places	28
2	Our carbon footprint	30
3	Past and present	32
4	Favourite fictional places	34
5	*The Lost City*	36
6	Unit 3 Revision	38
	My global progress	39

UNIT 4 Celebrations
1	Describing celebrations	40
2	The Rio Carnival	42
3	Personal celebrations	44
4	Favourite things	46
5	*Horrid Henry's Birthday party*	48
6	Unit 4 Revision	50
	My global progress	51

UNIT 5 Famous people
1	Professions	52
2	Famous people and their work	54
3	A presentation about a famous person	56
4	A short biography	58
5	Extracts from *The Stowaway*	60
6	Unit 5 Revision	62
	My global progress	63

UNIT 6 Myths and fables
1	Understanding myths and legends	64
2	Fables	66
3	Telling an anecdote	68
4	Lessons in life	70
5	*The Lambton Worm*	72
6	Unit 6 Revision	74
	My global progress	75

UNIT 7 Ancient civilisations
1	Ancient Egypt and Rome	76
2	Egyptian pyramids	78
3	Everyday life in ancient times	80
4	Discoveries	82
5	*There's a Pharaoh in Our Bath!*	84
6	Unit 7 Revision	86
	My global progress	87

UNIT 8 Weather and climate
1	Describing the weather	88
2	Rainforests	90
3	Extreme weather	92
4	Rainforest animals	94
5	*A visit with Mr Tree Frog* and *If I were a Sloth*	96
	Unit 8 Revision	98
	My global progress	99

UNIT 9 Planet Earth
1	Food chains	100
2	Animal camouflage	102
3	Looking after pets	104
4	Writing a leaflet	106
5	*Mum Won't Let Me Keep a Rabbit*	108
6	Unit 9 Revision	110
	My global progress	111

Talking about people

1 Describing people

1 Adjectives

Find and circle these adjectives.

~~cheerful~~ confident generous hardworking lazy nervous outgoing ~~selfish~~ shy tidy

N	V	Y	H	B	O	P	D	A	B	I	V	C
E	L	P	A	L	M	U	T	I	D	Y	O	S
R	G	R	R	N	C	C	T	J	X	N	R	C
V	E	E	D	N	O	H	P	G	F	L	R	U
O	N	A	W	U	N	E	G	I	O	Z	D	H
U	E	Q	O	C	F	E	D	L	C	I	S	N
S	R	O	R	E	I	R	G	U	F	I	N	Y
M	O	A	K	O	D	F	O	K	F	A	Z	G
N	U	Y	I	T	E	U	Y	L	M	A	Z	X
K	S	G	N	M	N	L	E	U	L	B	J	V
C	D	Q	G	U	T	S	O	O	S	H	Y	Z

2 Complete these sentences with an adjective from Activity 1.

1 I've got a test today. I'm feeling very ____nervous____ .

2 My grandma tells people I'm very _____ because I'm always studying.

3 My brother prefers watching the television to playing sport. He's so _____ .

4 My younger sister is really _____ . In fact, I think she's got more friends than I have and she's only six!

5 I'm very _____ , but my friends aren't! Their bedrooms are really messy!

Cambridge Global English Stage 5 Activity Book Unit 1

3 Antonyms

Find and match the adjectives to their opposite meaning.

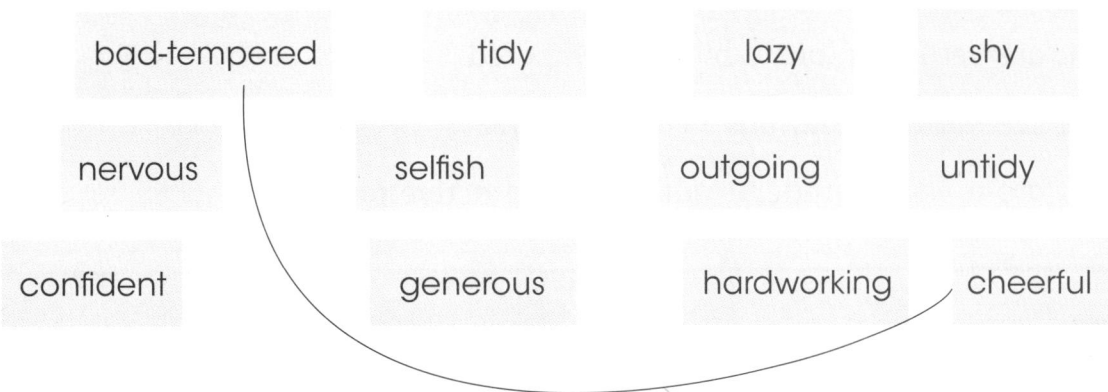

Strategy check! Reading for gist
Tick the strategies that will help you to read a text for gist. Use the strategies before you read the text below.

- Look at pictures. ☐
- Read the text quickly to find out what the topic is or the writer's feelings. ☐
- Read the whole text in detail. ☐
- Read the text quickly for the general meaning. ☐

4 Read the school report below. Circle the picture of the boy described in the report. Do you think Juan's parents are going to be happy with it?

Pupil: Juan Marquez **Class:** 3 **Teacher:** Miss Ana Lopez

Juan has progressed quite well this year. He is a very polite, happy pupil and a very popular member of the class. However, he isn't as hardworking as other pupils in the class and sometimes forgets to do his homework. The presentation of his work is always excellent, but sometimes his marks aren't very good because he gets very nervous when we have an exam.

5 Which adjectives in Activity 3 describe Juan's personality?

2 Our profiles

1 **Read** the profiles and match them to the correct summary below.

1 You are very tidy, but a bit bad-tempered.

2 You are hardworking and very confident.

3 You are a very confident, outgoing and active person.

Profile 1

Hi, my name's Lucia and I'm eleven years old. I'm from Tierra del Fuego, the 'Land of Fire', in Argentina. I've got two brothers, one is younger than me and the other is older. We get on really well together because we all love sport. I'm the captain of the girls' basketball team at school. I've got lots of friends, and I've got a pet lizard called Bruno and a cat called Silke. _____

Profile 2

Hello, I'm Tasanee and I'm from Thailand. I live with my parents and my brother and sister in the Samut Prakan Province about 30 kilometres south of Bangkok. I'm twelve years old and I love listening to pop music on the radio and reading cartoon books. At school I enjoy helping my teacher and classmates to organise the classroom. We sweep and mop the classroom floor, recycle materials and give out homework to our classmates. I get a bit angry when someone forgets their homework, so perhaps I should be a teacher when I grow up! _____

Profile 3

Hello there! I'm Sam and I'm from Bristol in England. I'm twelve years old and I'm an only child. I've got lots of pets. My parrot's name is Ariel, and I've got a hamster too, called Fluffy. I love playing with them both. I'm studying a lot at the moment because I've got a Maths and an English test this week. I'm sure I'm going to get top marks just like in the last exam. My hobbies are reading and training my parrot to talk! _____

2 Use of English

Make questions from the words below and answer them with information from the texts in Activity 1.

> **Use of English**
>
> **Question words with Wh-**
> What? Who? Where?
> When? Which? Whose? Why?

1 pets / What / has / got / Lucia _What pets has Lucia got_ ?
  She's got a dog called Bruno and a cat called Silke .

2 like / What / Lucia / is / _____ ?
  _____ .

3 Tasanee / is / Where / from _____ ?
  _____ .

4 people / Who / in / Tanasee's / are / the / family _____ ?
  _____ .

5 old / How / Sam / is _____ ?
  _____ .

6 Sam's / are / What / hobbies _____ ?
  _____ .

3 Write

Complete your profile.

Name:	Age:
Country:	Family:
Hobbies:	Pets:
Personality:	

 **Challenge**

4 Interview your partner. Take notes in your notebook and then write sentences about his/her life. Use the questions in Activity 2 as a guide.

My classmate's name is ...

Cambridge Global English Stage 5 Activity Book Unit 1

3 An interview

Strategy check! Listen for specific information
Tick the strategies that will help you to listen for specific information.
Use the strategies before you read the text below.
- Listen to the recording, but don't read the text first. ☐
- Read the text first and think about the type of words that are missing. ☐
- When you listen again, focus on the answers you have written. ☐
- Read the completed text to check it makes sense. ☐

56 1 Listen and complete the dialogue between the two children.

Hiro: Hello, my name's Hiro. What's yours?

Ben: Hi, I'm Ben. Where are you from?

Hiro: I'm from [1] _Tokyo_ . And you?

Ben: I'm from New York. Have you got any [2] _____ ?

Hiro: Yes, I've got an older brother. And you?

Ben: I'm an [3] _____

Hiro: Sorry, could you repeat that?

Ben: Yes, there's just me. I haven't got any brothers or sisters.

Hiro: Do you have a favourite sport?

Ben: Yes, **I really like** playing [4] _____ .

Hiro: Me too! Well, **I'm not so keen on** baseball, but I love playing table tennis!

Ben: What are you [5] _____ ?

Hiro: Well, **I think** I'm quite [6] _____ and cheerful, but my mum doesn't think so. She thinks I'm a bit lazy. Not true, of course!

Ben: Ha, ha!! Just like my mum! I'm quite hardworking, but Mum says I spend too much time playing computer games!

Hiro: Well, **we both like** playing computer games then. Which one is your favourite?

8 Cambridge Global English Stage 5 Activity Book Unit 1

2 Find an expression highlighted in the dialogue which ...

1 asks again _____

2 expresses likes _____

3 expresses dislike _____

4 compares _____

5 expresses an opinion _____

3 Write
Complete these sentences about yourself.

1 I really like _____ .

2 I'm not very keen on _____ .

3 I'm not sure if _____ .

4 It makes me angry when _____ .

5 I don't think _____ .

57 4 Pronunciation Intonation in question forms
Read the pronunciation guide. Listen and practise saying the questions.

- **Wh-** questions have a rising-falling intonation:
  What are you like?
- Yes/No questions usually end with a rising intonation:
  Do you have a favourite sport?

1 What are you like?
2 Where are you from?
3 Do you like playing computer games?
4 Are you outgoing?

5 Challenge Do a group survey

Get into groups of four and ask questions from Activity 1 to the people in your group. Make notes. Find the classmate who is most similar to yourself and present your findings to the class. Use expressions from Activity 2.

We both really like ...

Cambridge Global English Stage 5 Activity Book Unit 1

4 Favourite things

1 Read and match the headings to Natalie du Toit's *My Page*.

Personality: ~~City/country~~:   Family: Best feeling: Favourite place:

Advice to others: A dream come true

At the age of 14, Natalie du Toit, a talented South African swimmer, lost her leg in a motorcycle accident. Despite her disability, Natalie was determined to continue swimming and competing. Since then, she has won gold medals in the Paralympics and competed in the Beijing Olympic Games.

my blog   friends   photos   links

Name: Natalie du Toit
Date of birth: 29th January 1984

1 _City/country_ : Cape Town, South Africa
2 _____ : André du Toit (brother).
3 _____ : positive and determined.
4 _____ : swimming in the pool. I feel fantastic in the water!
5 _____ : Table Mountain in Cape Town – it's incredible!
6 _____ : competing in the Olympic Games. Wow!
7 _____ : be everything you want to be.

2 Use of English
Circle the adjective which best describes how she feels about the following things.

1 I feel **relaxed** / **relaxing** when I am with my two dogs.
2 Swimming in the pool is **exhilarating** / **exhilarated**.
3 Table Mountain in Cape Town is **amazed** / **amazing**!
4 Competing in the Olympic Games was so **excited** / **exciting**!

> **Use of English**
>
> **-ed / -ing adjectives**
>
> **-ed** adjectives such as **relaxed** and **amazed** are used to describe how people feel.
>
> **-ing** adjectives such as **exciting** and **exhilarating** are used to describe things and situations.

3 Write

Choose the correct form of the adjectives to complete the sentences.

> frightening / frightened
> bored / boring
> interesting / interested
> exciting / excited

1 Tidying up my bedroom is really _____ .

2 I am very _____ of horses.

3 I'm really _____ because I'm going to see Taylor Swift in concert!

4 I'm learning to play the guitar – it's really _____ !

5 I get _____ when I've got no friends to play with.

4 Complete these sentences. Use **-ing** and **-ed** adjectives.

1 My favourite thing is _____ . It's _____ .

2 My favourite animals are _____ . They make me feel _____ .

3 My favourite sport is _____ . It's _____ .

4 My favourite film is _____ . It's _____ .

5 I feel _____ when I _____ .

6 When I go to _____ on holiday. I feel _____ .

5 **Challenge**

Write a *My Page* in your notebook for your favourite famous person. Find out information about him/her on the Internet or in a magazine. Cut out photos from magazines.

Cambridge Global English Stage 5 Activity Book Unit 1

5 My favourite people

1 **Read** the poems *Super Samson Simpson* and *Our teacher's multi-talented* in the Learner's Book again and decide if the sentences are **T (true)** or **F (false)**. Correct the false sentences in your notebook.

Super Samson Simpson

1 Super Samson Simpson carries his grandma all day long.
   <u>F. He carries elephants all day long</u>.

2 His muscles are very big. _____

3 He can lift two dozen elephants. _____

4 He is the strongest in the Simpson family. _____

Our teacher's multi-talented

5 He's a brilliant dancer. _____

6 The teacher speaks twelve languages. _____

7 He's great at racing cars. _____

8 He always combs his hair. _____

2 **Vocabulary**
Complete the sentences with a word from the box.

Machine Man is the new superhero for kids. He can pick up a ¹ _dozen_ cars with one hand and ² _____ them in the air.

His muscles are ³ _____ and his legs are bionic, but these aren't his only talents. He's a ⁴ _____ skier and he ⁵ _____ with tigers. He also paints really ⁶ _____ pictures which are on display at the City Gallery.

| champion |
| wrestles |
| ~~dozen~~ |
| impressive |
| hoists |
| enormous |

Use of English

Changing adjectives into nouns
By adding *-th* to some adjectives and taking out or changing some letters, we can change them into nouns.
wide → width

3 Find the noun in the poems for the adjective strong.

strong _____

4 Match these adjectives to the correct noun.

1 wide   a length

2 long   b depth

3 deep   c width

5 Complete Machine Man's profile. Use information from Activity 2.

Physical qualities	Talents
_____	_____
_____	_____
_____	_____
_____	_____

6 Write a poem about Machine Man. Use the information from his profile.

Machine Man

His muscles _____ ,

His legs _____ too.

He's a champion _____ ,

And he _____ too.

Cambridge Global English Stage 5 Activity Book Unit 1   13

6 Unit 1 Revision

1 Multiple-choice quiz

1 My brother is _____ . He never shares anything with me!
   a generous   b lazy   c selfish

2 When my friend is _____ she bites her nails.
   a outgoing   b nervous   c bad-tempered

3 I am _____ that I can pass the exam.
   a shy   b confident   c hardworking

4 I'm not very _____ on playing basketball.
   a quite   b keen   c like

5 We _____ like playing table tennis.
   a too   b bit   c both

6 I'm not _____ if I can go to the party on Saturday.
   a sure   b keen   c like

7 I'm really _____ of spiders.
   a frightening   b frighten   c frightened

8 The book I am reading is very _____ .
   a interested   b interesting   c interest

9 Last night, the fireworks display was _____ !
   a interested   b amazed   c amazing

10 I love _____ the violin.
   a play   b playing   c played

11 Luis won a gold medal in the swimming race. He's a _____ swimmer!
   a great at   b champion   c quite

My global progress

Think about what you have studied in this unit. Answer the questions below.

1 What topics did you like and why?
　_____
　_____

2 What activities did you like and why?
　_____
　_____

3 What did you find challenging and why?
　_____
　_____

4 What help do you need now?
　_____
　_____

5 What would you like to find out more about?
　_____
　_____

6 What topics and activities relate to other subjects at your school?
　_____
　_____

Cambridge Global English Stage 5 Activity Book Unit 1

15

2 Staying healthy

1 Common illnesses

1 Vocabulary

Categorise the words. Write the symptoms next to the correct illness.

> ~~a sore throat~~   tummy hurts   a cold   a headache   blocked nose
> runny nose   a fever   stomach ache   no energy   sweating
> ~~lost voice~~   feel sick   shivering   head hurts   a cough   chesty cough

Illness	Symptoms
a sore throat	lost voice

2 Collocations

Read the sick notes and circle the correct words.

Dear Mrs Perkins,
Natasha won't be in school today because she's ¹(got)/ feels a headache and she ²feels / got sick. She ³hasn't got / feels a fever, so I hope she will be back at school tomorrow.
From,
Natasha's dad

Dear Mr Pranesh,
Mohammed isn't feeling well today. He ⁴feels / has got a stomach ache and he ⁵has got / feels sick. He ⁶has got / feels no energy and he ⁷'s got / is shivering a lot too. I hope he will be back at school on Monday.
From,
Mohammed's mum

16   Cambridge Global English Stage 5 Activity Book Unit 2

3 Dialogues

Complete the dialogues using the words from the box. Then match to the correct picture below.

| head hurts   ~~headache~~   sick |

1 A: What's the matter?
   B: I've got a ¹_____headache_____ .
   A: Do you feel ²_____ ?
   B: No, only my ³_____ .

| hot   sweating   fever |

2 A: What's the matter?
   B: I feel ¹_____ .
   A: Have you got a ²_____ ?
   B: Yes, I'm ³_____ .

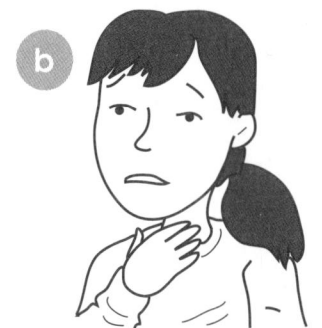

| sore throat   voice   headache |

3 A: What's the matter? Have you got a
      ¹_____ ?
   B: No, I've got a ²_____ .
      I can't talk because I've lost my
      ³_____ .

4 Challenge

Write your own dialogue. Use these prompts to help you.

| stomach ache   feel sick   no energy |

_____
_____
_____

Cambridge Global English Stage 5 Activity Book Unit 2   17

2 Fever

> **Strategy check!** Making predictions
> Tick the strategies that will help you to make predictions. Use the strategies before you read the text below.
> - Look at pictures. ☐
> - Read the whole text in detail. ☐
> - Look at the type of text (magazine article, leaflet ...). ☐

1 **Read** and choose the best title for the article.

a A stomach upset   b The flu   c Non-stop sneezing!

Have you ever had a fever, a bad cough, a headache and an aching body all at once? Well, if you have, then you've probably had the flu at some time in your life!

Flu, which is another name for *Influenza*, is caused by a virus and it's common, especially in the winter months. You might think you have a cold instead of the flu because **many** of the symptoms can be quite similar, such as a runny nose, sneezing and coughing, but children with the flu often have a fever and headaches. You don't feel like eating **much** food either and all your body hurts. The flu can last a week or more.

Catching the flu is very easy. If you are near a person with the flu, who sneezes, coughs or even laughs, then the tiny drops that come out of their mouth can infect you if you breathe them in.

So, how can you protect yourself from getting the flu? First of all, keep your distance from someone with the flu! Wash your hands regularly with hot water and soap, and don't put your hands to your mouth or nose.

If you catch the flu, you should get **a lot of** rest and drink **plenty of** liquids, such as water, juice and soups. You can take **some** medicine too, but only if your mum or doctor gives it you to help with your fever and headaches.

2 Read the text again. Use coloured pens to underline;
<u>Blue</u>: three illnesses
<u>Red</u>: four symptoms
<u>Green</u>: advice given if you have the flu.

18 Cambridge Global English **Stage 5 Activity Book Unit 2**

3 Use of English
Circle the correct answer. Use the information in the table to help you.

1 Don't eat **many** / **much** food if you have a fever.

2 Wash your hands with water and **a few** / **a little** soap.

3 You need **much** / **plenty** of tissues if you have a cold.

4 If you have **any** / **some** medicine, you will feel better.

5 How **much** / **many** days does the flu last?

6 Can I have **any** / **some** cough medicine, please?

Use of English

Quantifiers
A quantifier expresses quantity.
Countable: a few, many, several
You will experience **many** symptoms.
Uncountable: much, some, any, little
Some families have little money.
Both: no, a lot of, plenty of
There are **a lot of** / **plenty of** vaccines.

---

4 Use the five quantifiers highlighted in the text in Activity 1 to complete these sentences.

1 There are __a lot of__ cases of flu in the winter.

2 You shouldn't eat _____ , but you should drink _____ water if you have a fever.

3 _____ people suffer from a sore throat in the winter.

4 You should take _____ medicine if your temperature rises to more than 37.5C.

5 Challenge
Complete these sentences for you. Write two examples of your own using quantifiers.

1 When I have a cold, __I use a lot of tissues__ .

2 When I have a cough, I _____ .

3 When I have the flu, I _____ .

4 When I have a headache, I _____ .

5 _____

6 _____

Cambridge Global English Stage 5 Activity Book Unit 2

3 Food and health

1 **Read**
   Do the food quiz.

① **What nutrients do we need in a healthy diet?**
   a Proteins, carbohydrates, vitamins, minerals and fats.
   b Fats, proteins and sugar.
   c Minerals and vitamins.

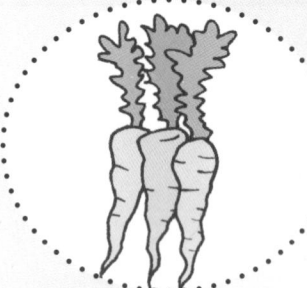

② **Which of these foods contain most protein?**
   a tomatoes
   b carrots
   c eggs

③ **Why is calcium important?**
   a Because it helps build strong muscles.
   b Because it keeps our bones and teeth healthy.
   c Because it provides us with minerals.

④ **Which foods are carbohydrates?**
   a Sweets, cakes and oils.
   b Bread, rice and pasta.
   c Vegetables, fruit and nuts.

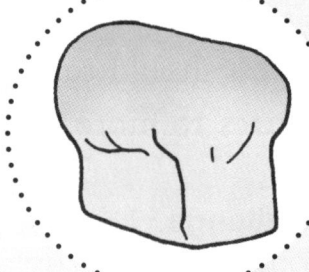

⑤ **Which is the healthiest snack?**
   a sweets
   b cakes
   c fruit
   d chips

⑥ **Why are green vegetables so important in our diet?**
   a They keep our teeth healthy.
   b They contain a lot of minerals and vitamins.
   c They look good on the plate!

2 Categorise the food.

chocolate   rice   pasta   ~~eggs~~   bread   cheese   oil   fish   nuts   lettuce
carrots   chicken   milk   apples   bananas   oranges   green beans   onion

Proteins	Carbohydrates	Vitamins and minerals	Fats and sugars
eggs			

3 Use of English

Complete the sentences with **should** or **shouldn't**, plus a verb from the box.

try   spend   put   exercise   drink   ~~eat~~

Use of English

should/shouldn't
You **should** eat fruit as a nutritious snack.
We **shouldn't** eat chocolates and sweets every day.

1 We ____should eat____ fruit and vegetables every day because they provide our bodies with vitamins and minerals.

2 You _____ to eat lots of different types of food.

3 Katie _____ so much butter on her bread.

4 You _____ often to keep healthy.

5 The dentist said I _____ too many fizzy drinks.

6 Lucas _____ so much time watching TV.

4 Challenge

Write sentences in your notebook about the food you eat on a typical day.

On a typical day, I usually eat cereal for breakfast. Cereals have carbohydrates, and there is calcium in the milk. For lunch …

4 Health blogs

1 Vocabulary
Do the health crossword.

Down ↓

1 You have this to check you can see well.
2 An injection to protect you from disease.
3 When a part of your body feels itchy and red you may have a … .
4 You have this to check you can hear well.
5 A piece of paper with details of the medicine that someone needs.

Across →

6 When your ear hurts you may have an … .
7 When you push air from the lungs with a short loud sound.

2 **Read** and match the descriptions to the health problem.

> a sore throat   an allergic reaction   a chest infection

my blog friends photos links

1 Dear Doctor,

When I drink and eat, it really hurts to swallow and my neck hurts too.

What should I do? _____

2 Dear Doctor,

Despite feeling OK during the day, I can't sleep at night because I cough all the time. I'm drinking a lot of fluids, but I'm not getting better.

What should I do? _____

3 Dear Doctor,

Before I went to school this morning I looked in the mirror and I had red spots all over my arms, tummy and face. They are very itchy!

What should I do? _____

3 **Writing tip** Contrast linkers
Complete the sentences with words from the box. Some words can be used more than once.

> despite
> although
> in spite of

1 I cough all night, ___*despite*___ feeling OK during the day.

2 I went to school, _____ the red spots all over my body.

3 _____, I'm drinking a lot of fluids, I'm not getting better.

4 _____ taking the medicine, it still really hurts to swallow.

4 **Challenge**
Imagine you are a doctor. Write advice for one of the children with a health problem in Activity 2. Remember to use **should** and **shouldn't** to give advice.

_____

_____

Cambridge Global English Stage 5 Activity Book Unit 2   23

5 Stone soup

1   **Read** the story *Stone soup* again. Order the sentences which summarise the story.

   a   On the day he ran out of money and food he came across a village. _____

   b   The woman from the first house he had asked for food gave him some mushrooms and herbs. _____

   c   No-one in the village had any food at all. _____

   d   He knocked at the door of all the houses in the village asking for a little food. _____

   e   The young man told the elderly man that he wanted to make the villagers a big pot of soup from the special stone he had found on his travels because no-one had any food. _____

   f   He asked the old man for a little onion and some cabbage. _____

   g   The elderly man gave him a large pot of water and a stirring spoon   _6_

   h   A little girl gave the young man some salt and pepper and a bowl of beans to put in the soup. _____

   i   Once there was a young man travelling the country selling his goods.   _1_

   j   Everyone has a delicious bowl of soup. _____

   k   The old man's neighbour gave the young man a chunk of meat, a bunch of carrots and a sack of potatoes to add flavour to the soup. _____

2   Circle the correct words.

   1   The villagers **had / didn't** have food.

   2   The stone **was / wasn't** magic.

   3   The villagers **wanted / didn't want** to help a stranger.

   4   The young man **persuaded / didn't persuade** the villagers to give him ingredients for the soup.

   5   The young man **wasn't / was** very clever.

24   Cambridge Global English Stage 5 Activity Book Unit 2

3 Vocabulary Classifying expressions
Label the food with the correct expression.

> a bag of   a pinch of   a bunch of   ~~a sack of~~   a head of   a bowl of

a sack of potatoes _____ _____ _____ _____ _____

58 4 Pronunciation Connected speech
Listen and repeat the mini-dialogues. Which words are not pronounced clearly?

1 **A:** What fruit did you buy?

   B: I bought a bunch of grapes and a bag of oranges.

2 **A:** What would you like for lunch?

   B: A bowl of soup please, and some bread and butter.

3 **A:** Should I add some salt and pepper to the soup?

   B: Yes please, but not too much salt.

5 Values Helping each other
Circle the correct option for you.

1 I **always / sometimes / never** make my bed in the morning.

2 I **always / sometimes / never** recycle rubbish.

3 I **always / sometimes / never** give my seat to an elderly person on a bus.

4 I **always / sometimes / never** help my friends if they are upset about something.

6 Challenge

In your notebook, write more examples of how you help others at home, at school or in your community.

6 Unit 2 Revision

1 Vocabulary
Match the sentence halves.

1 When I've got a cold,   a I sometimes lose my voice.
2 When I eat too much,   b I feel dizzy.
3 When I have a sore throat,   c provide our bodies with calcium.
4 When I have a fever,   d I usually have a runny nose.
5 When I have a headache,   e provide our bodies with proteins.
6 Potatoes and rice   f I shiver a lot.
7 Eggs, meat and fish   g give us energy.
8 Dairy products   h I feel sick.

2 Use of English
Read and circle the correct answer.

If you catch the flu you ¹**should / shouldn't** rest as much as possible. The symptoms you might have are headaches, a blocked nose and a fever. You'll probably have ²**a few / little** energy to do all the things you usually do, and your body will hurt ³**a lot / many**. If you take ⁴**some / any** medicine, it will help you feel a bit better. You ⁵**should / shouldn't** eat ⁶**many / much** food if you have a fever, but be sure to drink ⁷**several / plenty** of fluids.

3 Over to you
Complete these sentences about your diet.

1 I usually eat _____ for breakfast.
2 I always eat _____ for a snack.
3 I never eat _____ for lunch.
4 I sometimes eat _____ for lunch.
5 I often eat _____ for dinner.
6 I usually eat _____ before I go to bed.

4 Write sentences about the food you should and shouldn't eat in your diet and why.

My global progress

Think about what you have studied in this unit. Answer the questions below.

1 What topics did you like and why?
   _____
   _____

2 What activities did you like and why?
   _____
   _____

3 What did you find challenging and why?
   _____
   _____

4 What help do you need now?
   _____
   _____

5 What would you like to find out more about?
   _____
   _____

6 What topics and activities relate to other subjects at your school?
   _____
   _____

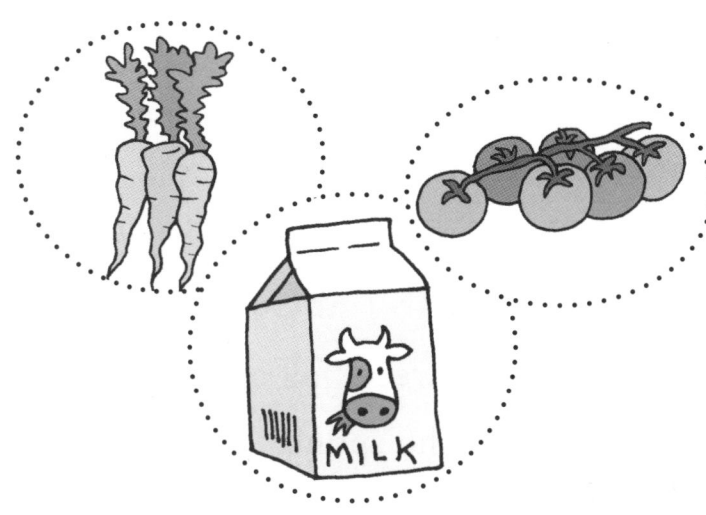
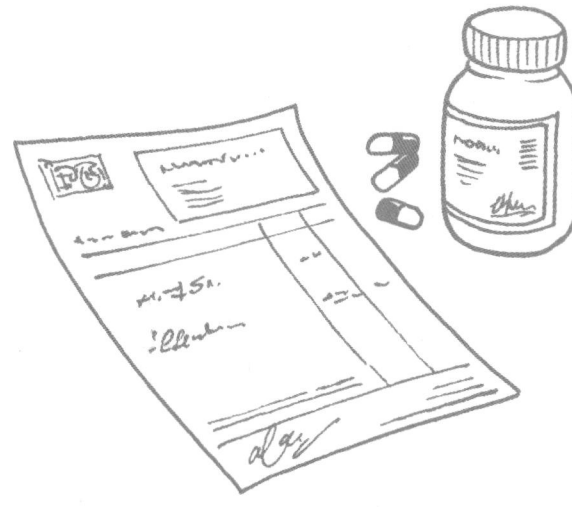

Cambridge Global English Stage 5 Activity Book Unit 2   27

3 Where we live

1 Describing places

1 Vocabulary
Complete the words.

1 r o a d
2 v e h i c l e
3 _ _ i c _
4 b _ _ l _ _ g
5 p _ e _ _ _ _

6 _ a _ _
7 l _ _ _
8 _ _ r _
9 _ _ i _ d

2 Circle the adjectives which best describe the city or the country.

1 Living in the country is **noisy** / **peaceful** / **crowded**.
2 Cities are very **clean** / **popular** / **small** places to live.
3 If you live in the country you breathe **dirty** / **fresh** / **noisy** air.
4 Cities have **ancient** / **crowded** / **spectacular** streets full of people.
5 The country is **modern** / **small** / **beautiful** in the spring.

3 Read

Study the text about visiting Buenos Aires in Argentina. Write the adjective in the brackets in its comparative or superlative form.

Use of English

Comparatives and superlatives
The city is **dirtier than** the country.
The country is **more peaceful than** the city.
It is **the biggest** city in India.
It has got **the most spectacular** mountains.

ARGENTINA

Buenos Aires is one of Latin America's ¹ _largest_ (large) cities. It is near the East coast of Argentina and has a population of about 13 million. It is one of the ² _____ (beautiful) cities in Latin America with great cafés and lovely buildings.

■ Best time to travel

If you are planning to visit Argentina, the ³ _____ (good) time to go is in the autumn or the spring when the weather is good. In the winter, it is ⁴ _____ (cold) than in the autumn, and in the summer, it is ⁵ _____ (hot) and ⁶ _____ (humid) than the other months of the year.

■ Getting around

Traffic in Buenos Aires is ⁷ _____ (heavy) than in other Latin America cities, so the best way to travel around is to either walk or to use the metro or subte which is a ⁸ _____ (fast) and ⁹ _____ (cheap) way to travel.

■ Things to see

Don't leave Buenos Aires without going to Palermo Zoo to see the 300 animals. Or visit the Parque de la Costa the ¹⁰ _____ (big) amusement park in South America!

4 Challenge

Compare your city or town to Buenos Aires in Argentina, using comparatives and superlatives. Think about size, weather and things to see.

My city is smaller than Buenos Aires.

Cambridge Global English Stage 5 Activity Book Unit 3

2 Our carbon footprint

Strategy check! Scanning
Tick the strategies that will help you to scan.
- Read the whole text in detail. ☐
- Look at the pictures to help you. ☐
- Read the text quickly in order to locate information. ☐

1 **Read** the text and find two reasons why it's important to plant trees.

Tree facts
- Trees can live for thousands of years.
- Trees produce oxygen and reduce the amount of carbon dioxide in the atmosphere.
- One large tree can provide a day's oxygen for up to four people.

Plant a tree and change the future!

Did you know that planting trees is a great way to help the environment? Trees release oxygen into the air, making our air cleaner, so, in many countries, people are planting trees.

South America

Latin America has the world's largest tropical forest – the Amazon. It has 57 per cent of the world's forests. So, children at an elementary school in El Trapiche, Argentina are learning about climate change and energy efficiency, and have been planting trees.

Since the programme was launched in December 2008, 200 000 trees have been planted in 22 towns across the central province of San Luis.

The UK

The Woodland Trust started a 'More Trees, More Good' campaign. They want to plant six million trees over the next 50 years. Schools and businesses are all helping because they know how important it is to plant more trees. Noah, from Birchanger Primary School helped plant over 50 trees at his school with his friends and teachers. 'It was great fun planting the trees – we all wore our wellies and got muddy!'

Why plant trees?
- To make homes for animals.
- To make the countryside look beautiful.
- To help us make a greener world.

2 Circle the correct answer.

1 If we plant more trees there's **more carbon dioxide / less carbon dioxide** in the atmosphere.

2 If we plant more trees **the air is cleaner / there is less oxygen**.

3 The Amazon is home to **half / more than half** the world's forests.

4 Children have planted **twenty thousand / two hundred thousand** trees in San Luis since 2008.

5 Noah **enjoyed / didn't enjoy** planting the trees at his school.

3 Use of English
Underline the subordinate clause in each sentence.

1 She decided to plant the tree <u>because it would help the environment</u>.

2 The children hope that their campaign will help the environment.

3 Scientists know that planting more trees produces more oxygen for us to breathe.

> ## Use of English
>
> **Subordinate clauses**
> A subordinate clause is a group of words with a subject and a verb that cannot stand alone as a sentence.
>
> … and some scientists believe that **this is making Earth hotter**.
> Schools and businesses are all helping **because they know how important it is to plant more trees**.

4 Make true sentences for you. Use the words in the box.

| believe   know   hope   think |

1 I _____ that we can reduce global warming.

2 I _____ that glaciers are melting.

3 I _____ that we should plant more trees.

4 I _____ that we should walk and cycle more instead of using the car.

Cambridge Global English Stage 5 Activity Book Unit 3   31

3 Past and present

Strategy check! Identifying opinions
Tick the sentences that express opinions.
- I prefer travelling by bus than by car. ☐
- We can't take mobile phones to school. ☐
- I really like the old buses in my town. ☐
- You should always cross the road on a zebra crossing. ☐

59 1 Listen to Cheung describe his city in the past and the present. Match the sentence halves. There are two items you don't need.

1 I don't think   a going out with my friends.

2 In my opinion,   b life was very easy in the past.

3 I really like   c playing sport.

                          d we should ride our bikes more.

4 I think that   e living in Beijing now is probably better than 100 years ago.

                          f big families should all live together again.

59 2 Vocabulary
Listen and tick the appliances Cheung mentions. Then write the words under the pictures.

3 Use of English

Match the present and the past simple of the verbs.

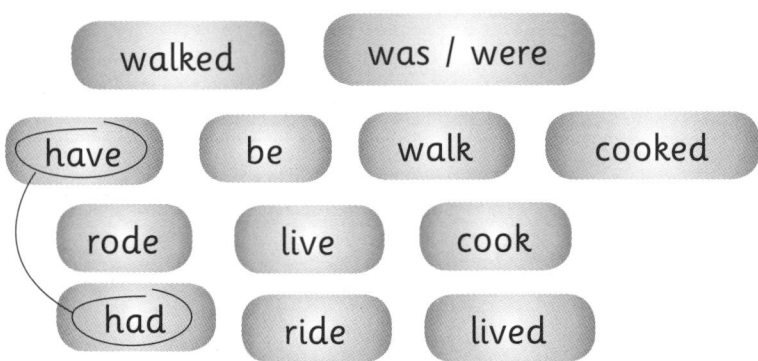

> **Use of English**
>
> **Past simple regular and irregular verbs**
> People **cooked** on a stove. They **didn't use** washing machines.
> **Irregular verbs:** We don't add **-ed** to these verbs in the past simple.
> **have:** had **be:** was/were
> **go:** went **drive:** drove.

4 Complete the sentences with the correct form of the verb.

1 I ___didn't___ have (*not have*) a bicycle until I was five.

2 My father _____ (*walk*) to school when he _____ (*be*) a child.

3 There _____ (*not be*) any modern cookers when my grandmother was little.

4 My mum _____ (*ride*) her bike to school when she was a child.

5 People _____ (*live*) in big houses with all the family.

6 People _____ (*not use*) mobile phones.

5 Complete the text with the correct form of the verbs in brackets.

| not drive   walk   work   ride   not have (x2)   not be   ~~live~~ |

In the past, people ¹ ___lived___ in houses with all the members of their family. The houses ² _____ running water or bathrooms. People often ³ _____ in the countryside in the fields and they ⁴ _____ cars – they ⁵ _____ everywhere. To get around cities, people ⁶ _____ their bicycles. They ⁷ _____ the modern appliances we have today and there ⁸ _____ any high-rise office buildings or apartment blocks.

4 Favourite fictional places

1 Vocabulary

Look and write the adjectives below the picture they best describe.

huge   magical   mysterious   exciting   scary-looking   enchanting

a

b

_____   _____

_____   _____

_____   _____

2 Substitute the words in bold with an adjective with a similar meaning from Activity 1.

1 The volcano was **very big**. _huge_

2 The enormous birds were **frightening**. _____

3 It was a **very nice** place with lush, green hills. _____

4 Lord Black wore a **curious** black cape. _____

5 The trees are **special** because they grow lollipops and sweets. _____

6 The film was **full of action**. _____

3 **Read** and match the description to the correct picture.

1 Londorf is a dark, **scary** place at the end of the earth. The only inhabitants of this **desolate** place are King Londorf, his army of beasts and a flock of **gigantic**, black crows.

2 The dark clouds hide the light of the **pale** sun and only the lava from the erupting volcanoes light up this dark, **miserable** place. The only other animals that survive in this place are **strange** lizard-like creatures, which live between the rocks and stones.

3 I definitely wouldn't want to visit or live in this place, and I certainly wouldn't want to meet the army of beasts in King Londorf's castle!

4 Answer these questions about the paragraphs above.

1 Which paragraph expresses the opinion of the writer?
2 Which paragraph talks about the location?
3 Which paragraph describes the place?

5 Answer the questions about the texts in Activity 3.

1 What lives on Londorf? _____
2 What can you see in the sky? _____
3 Would you like to visit this place? Why? Why not? _____
_____

6 Match the words in bold from the Activity 3 texts to the words below.

1 sad _miserable_
2 curious _____
3 frightening _____
4 very big _____
5 a faint colour _____
6 a bleak and lonely place _____

7 **Challenge**

In your notebook draw a picture of your favourite fictional place. Think of adjectives to describe it and organise your writing into three paragraphs.

5 The Lost City

1 Read *The Lost City* again and match each sentence to the picture it describes.

1 'There it is! There is the Lost City! We have found it at last,' Ho-Shing said. _c_

2 'Look at their ruby eyes!' Yong-Hu said. 'Can I bang the gong?' ___

3 Yong-Hu and Ho-Shing walked through the valley. 'I'm getting tired,' Yong-Hu complained. ___

4 'We must climb these steps,' Ho-Shing said, pointing to very steep steps that led to the top of the wall. ___

2 Read and decide if these sentences are **T (true)** or **F (false)**. Correct the false sentences in your notebook.

1 Yong-Hu and Ho-Shing are pandas.	(T) / F
2 Yong-Hu knows more about the Lost City than Ho-Shing.	T / F
3 There is a lot of bamboo in the Lost City.	T / F
4 It takes a day to walk to the Lost City.	T / F
5 Yong-Hu runs up all of the stairs in one go.	T / F
6 The music of the crickets is Yong-Hu's surprise.	T / F

3 **Vocabulary**
   Complete each sentence with the correct word.

   1 Crickets and birds __chirp__ .
   2 A _____ is a precious red stone.
   3 The music of the crickets was the _____ for their journey.
   4 A _____ is the sound a lion makes.
   5 The roofs of the buildings _____ in the sunshine.

   ruby
   roar
   reward
   ~~chirp~~
   sparkle

4 Answer the questions about the text.

   1 Why does Ho-Shing want to find the Lost City?
   _____
   2 What do they hear on the way?
   _____
   3 How long does it take them to get there?
   _____
   4 What is special about the roofs of the buildings?
   _____
   5 What did the pandas find in the Lost City?
   _____

60 5 **Pronunciation -ed** Listen and circle the verb which sounds different.

   1 cooked   watched   started
   2 lived   played   needed
   3 painted   washed   talked

6 **Values** Looking after our environment
   Look at the pictures and write about the ways in which we can look after our environment.

Cambridge Global English **Stage 5** Activity Book Unit 3

6 Unit 3 Revision

1 Crossword

Read the clues and complete the crossword.

Across →

4 Very quiet.
5 When the air you breathe is clean.
7 When something looks frightening.
8 A lot of trees in a group.
9 Very big.

Down ↓

1 A machine that washes plates and cups.
2 Very old.
3 Something that you walk on next to the road.
6 We _____ paper and cartons in our school.
8 We use this to keep food and drink cool.

My global progress

Think about what you have studied in this unit. Answer the questions below.

1 What topics did you like and why?

2 What activities did you like and why?

3 What did you find challenging and why?

4 What help do you need now?

5 What would you like to find out more about?

6 What topics and activities relate to other subjects at your school?

4 Celebrations

1 Describing celebrations

1 Vocabulary

Find and circle nine celebration words in the word search.

C	O	S	T	U	M	E	S	C	F	U	D
N	T	G	O	C	D	K	Q	W	E	R	D
F	R	K	Q	T	E	L	Y	K	A	S	F
X	A	X	Z	A	C	A	D	S	S	S	I
I	D	R	L	L	O	N	Y	E	T	Y	R
C	I	P	O	W	R	T	I	M	P	M	E
N	T	A	J	L	A	E	A	U	M	B	W
G	I	R	H	I	T	R	Q	T	O	O	O
O	O	A	Q	G	I	N	A	S	Y	L	R
Q	N	D	D	H	O	S	O	O	B	M	K
N	S	E	N	T	N	I	G	C	R	Q	S
Z	R	S	M	S	S	E	Z	J	B	H	P

~~fireworks~~
feast
decorations
parades
lanterns
traditions
symbol
costumes
lights

2 Complete the sentences with a word from Activity 1.

1 The ___fireworks___ display is brilliant on New Year's Eve! They light up the night sky and make lots of noise.

2 What a _____ ! The food looks delicious.

3 The shamrock is the _____ of Saint Patrick's Day in Ireland.

4 We hang beautiful _____ from the windows during Diwali.

5 The carnival _____ through the streets of Rio de Janiero are the most spectacular in the world.

6 Every country and culture has different _____ and celebrations.

40 Cambridge Global English Stage 5 Activity Book Unit 4

3 **Problem solving**

Convert the clock times and write the time.

1 21:30

   It's half past nine.

2 17:45

3 04:15

4 18:25

5 23:45

6 00:35

4 Read the text and complete the notes about the festival.

The colourful festival of Holi is celebrated at the end of February, or early March, and lasts for a day. The festival has an ancient origin and celebrates that 'good' is better than 'bad'. Holi celebrations begin with lighting a bonfire on the eve of Holi. On Holi day people spray coloured water on each other with *pichkaris* (water pistols). The most enjoyable tradition of Holi is the tradition of breaking the pot. A pot of buttermilk is hung high on the streets. Men form a huge human pyramid and the man on the top breaks the pot with his head. People also eat and drink traditional things like *thandai* (a drink) or *pakoras* (fried vegetables), and they hug and wish each other 'Happy Holi'.

Name of festival	When celebrated?	What it celebrates?	How long?	How people celebrate?
Holi				

5 Challenge

Complete in your own words the description about a celebration you have been to.

Cambridge Global English Stage 5 Activity Book Unit 4   41

2 The Rio Carnival

Strategy check! Visualising a context
Tick the strategies that will help you visualise a context.
- Create a picture in your mind about what you are reading. ☐
- Use your imagination. ☐
- Look up all the words you don't understand. ☐

1 Read Marco's account of the carnival in his city. Visualise the context as you read and then tick the picture which matches the celebration.

---

my blog | friends | photos | links

Last week we celebrated Carnival (*Carnevale*) in my home town of Viareggio which is a seaside town in Italy. It is one of the biggest carnival celebrations in Italy and is famous for its giants' parade. The giants, which are made from *papier maché*, parade on their floats along the seafront promenade. It's really good fun and the giants are incredible!

We all dress up in our favourite fancy dress costumes and line the streets to watch the giants pass by. We throw confetti at them, which are small bits of coloured paper, and eat traditional food.

At night, after the parade, there is an amazing fireworks display to end the carnival celebration. This year, the fireworks display lasted 15 minutes! It was spectacular!

2 Use of English
Circle the correct answer.

1 Viareggio is a seaside town, **who / which** has a big Carnival celebration.

2 These are the costumes, **who / which** the children wear.

3 Those are the giants **that / who** parade along the seafront.

4 We throw confetti, **who / which** are small pieces of coloured paper.

5 There is a fireworks display, **which / who** ends the celebration.

> **Use of English**
>
> **Defining relative clauses**
> These give us important information about a noun or noun phrase.
> We don't use commas.
> We use **who** or **that** to talk about people.
> ... and tourists **who** come to watch the carnival too.
> We use **that** or **which** to talk about things.
> The amazing parade **which** takes place in the Sambódromo ...

3 Join these sentences with a defining relative clause.

1 That's the giant. I saw it yesterday.
<u>That's the giant, which I saw yesterday.</u>

2 That's the girl. She was the Carnival Queen.
_____

3 I stayed in a hotel. It was very expensive.
_____

4 Venice is a famous city in Italy. It also has a big carnival celebration.
_____

5 Those are the special cakes. We eat them during carnival.
_____

4 Challenge

Design and describe your own giant for the Carnival parade in your notebook.

3 Personal celebrations

1 **Read** the text and match each child to the correct information.

1 **Ana:** In Brazil, we pull the earlobe of the birthday boy or girl for the number of years they are celebrating.

2 **Ching Lan:** In China, we receive gifts of money from our family on our birthday. We also invite friends and family to eat noodles, which wish the birthday child a long life.

3 **Peter:** In Denmark, we fly a flag outside the window of our houses to announce that it's someone's birthday.

4 **Tom:** In England, we give our friends the 'bumps' on their birthday. We lift them in the air by their hands and feet and raise them up and down to the floor, one for each year and one for good luck.

5 **Mai:** In Vietnam, everyone celebrates their birthday on New Year's Day. They don't celebrate the exact day they were born. Children say they were born in the year of the symbol of the lunar calendar for that year.

6 **Kylie:** In the USA, it is traditional for the birthday child to blow out the candles on a birthday cake. The number of candles represents the number of years the child is celebrating. As they blow out the candles, it is traditional to make a wish.

1	Ana	a gets money for her birthday.
2	Ching Lan	b has a flag outside his house.
3	Peter	c lives in Brazil.
4	Tom	d blows out the candles on her birthday cake.
5	Mai	e celebrates her birthday on New Year's Day.
6	Kylie	f gets the 'bumps' on his birthday.

2 Answer the questions for you.

1 Do you have any of these birthday traditions in your culture? Which ones?

2 Which do you like?

Cambridge Global English **Stage 5** Activity Book Unit 4

3 Vocabulary

Complete the sentences with words from the box.

> lights   ~~food~~   blow out   get   cake   blessing   song

1 My mum prepares a lot of delicious __food__ for my birthday party.
2 I _____ a very big birthday _____ .
3 My mum _____ the candles.
4 My family and friends sing a traditional _____ on my birthday.
5 I _____ _____ the candles on my cake.
6 I receive a _____ .

Use of English

will

We use **will** to express what you believe or know will happen in the future. The contracted form is more common.
I'll (will) receive my first kimono.
My mum **will make** a big birthday cake.
I won't have a big party.

4 Use of English

Write questions and answers about Jack's next birthday.

1 have / party __Will Jack have a party?__   __No, he won't__ .
2 go / cinema _____   _____ .
3 get / presents _____   _____ .
4 have / special meal _____   _____ .
5 have / birthday cake _____   _____ .

5 Challenge

Write about how you will celebrate your next birthday.

For my next birthday, I'll probably _____
_____
_____

4 Favourite things

1 Read and write the name of the special food above each picture.

Ghana

Vietnam

(South) Korea

Harvest festival!

Did you know that there are harvest festivals all over the world? This festival celebrates the gathering of the crops. We eat all kinds of different foods around the globe, so each country celebrates with its own special food and recipes. Read on to find out more.

In Ghana, they celebrate the Yam festival (*Homowo*) which lasts for three days. The yam looks a bit like a potato, but it is longer and more pointed. It's a very important crop in Ghana and many special foods are made from it, such as mashed yams with boiled eggs.

In Korea, they give thanks to the harvest during *Chu Suk* with a special feast. Families prepare a dish called *Songphyun* which are crescent-shaped rice cakes made of rice, beans, sesame seeds and chestnuts. Women sing and dance, they also play a game called turtle tag.

In Vietnam, *Trung Thu* celebrates the harvest moon. It's also a time for parents to spend more time with their children. They eat a special type of food called mooncakes which are made of salted eggs, seeds, vegetables and oil. The children wear colourful masks and parade through the streets with different shaped lanterns.

2 Complete the sentences with the correct word.

1 In Ghana, they harvest the yams _and_ make many special foods from them.

2 In Korea, they have a special feast _____ .

3 During *Chu Suk* the women sing, dance and they _____ play a game called turtle tag.

4 _____ children and parents celebrate *Trung Thu*.

5 They wear colourful masks and parade through the streets _____ .

> also
> ~~and~~
> both
> as well
> too

3 Read the recipe for mashed yams with boiled eggs and match each instruction to the correct picture.

Ingredients:

2 cups mashed yams
2 teaspoons grated onions
1 cup of oil
1 ripe tomato
6 hard-boiled eggs
salt and pepper

1 Boil the yams.
2 Mash the yams with a fork.
3 Fry the onions in oil.
4 Add tomatoes.
5 Mash two egg yolks (the yellow part).
6 Mix the eggs, the onion and the oil.
7 Put the mixture in with the yams and mix well.
8 Decorate with the eggs that are left.

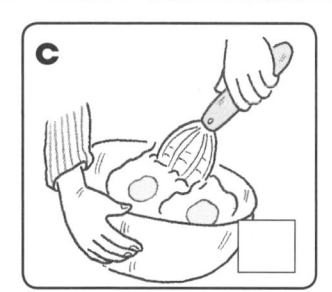

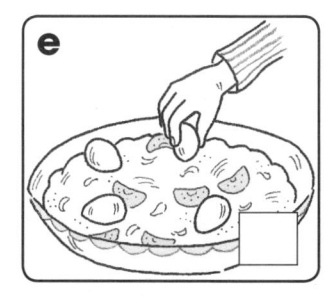

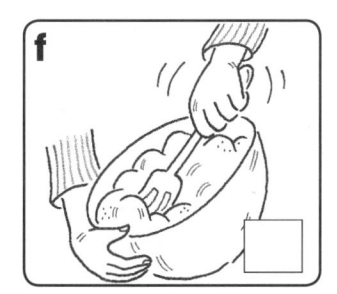

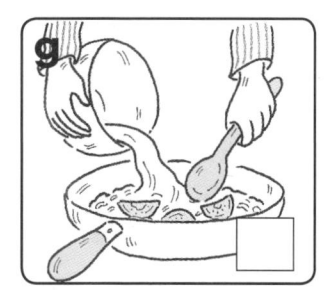

4 📝 **Challenge**

Draw and describe a food you like to eat during harvest festival.

5 Horrid Henry's Birthday Party

1 **Read** the extract again. Why doesn't he want these classmates to come to his party?

1 Margaret _Because she's too moody._
2 Susan _____
3 Andrew _____
4 Toby _____
5 William _____
6 Ralph _____

2 Unjumble the adjectives and match them to the classmates they describe on Henry's list. Use the text in the Learner's Book to help you.

Invitation list

Clever Clare   _____ Andrew
Moody Margaret   _____ Ralph
_____ Toby   _Jolly_ Josh
_____ William   _____ Graham

nxosuai
erdu
gohtu
eweyp
regyed

3 Decide which sentences are **fact (F)** or **opinion (O)**.

1 Andrew is no fun. _F_
2 I don't want any girls at all, thought Henry. ___
3 He crossed out Moody Margaret's name. ___
4 Ralph didn't invite Henry to his party. ___
5 He didn't want Peter to come to his party. ___
6 No horrid kids would be coming to his party. ___
7 No guests meant no presents. ___

48 Cambridge Global English Stage 5 Activity Book Unit 4

4 Read the clues and do the crossword.

Down ↓
1 Fun.
4 Not polite.
5 Not hardworking.
6 Strong.

Across →
2 Bad-tempered.
3 Intelligent.
7 Nervous.
8 Crying a lot.

5 Vocabulary Opposites

Write the opposite adjectives.

~~tough~~   anxious   bad-tempered   hardworking   rude   jolly

1 The giant wasn't weak. He was big and ___*tough*___ .

2 The boy is not polite: in fact, he is _____ . He never says **please** or **thank you** to anyone.

3 He isn't confident. He gets very _____ when he has an exam.

4 She's always angry – she never smiles. _____

5 She's such a _____ person. She's always smiling.

6 He's so _____ . He's always studying at his desk.

6 Pronunciation -ough

Listen and cross out the word which has a different sound.

1 tough   bought   enough

2 dough   rough   though

3 thought   bought   enough

Cambridge Global English Stage 5 Activity Book Unit 4

6 Unit 4 Revision

1 Multiple-choice quiz

Choose the correct word to complete the sentences.

1 On New Year's Eve, there are _____ displays in public places.
   a lights   b firework   c lantern

2 The dragon _____ through the streets during the Chinese New Year.
   a rides   b flies   c parades

3 The Rio de Janiero Carnival _____ for four days.
   a celebrates   b lasts   c takes place

4 A costume is something _____ people wear during a celebration.
   a who   b which   c where

5 Tourists _____ come to watch the Carnival are amazed!
   a that   b who   c which

6 I will _____ my coming of age when I am 21.
   a receive   b make   c celebrate

7 I _____ be a year older next year.
   a am   b won't   c will

8 I celebrate my birthdays with _____ my family and friends.
   a both   b too   c as well

9 You need to add sugar to the cake mixture _____ .
   a and   b both   c too

10 William is so _____ . He cries all the time!
   a anxious   b clever   c weepy

11 Your son needs to be more polite in class. Sometimes he is very _____ .
   a miserable   b lazy   c rude

12 She can be very _____ at times. She shuts herself in her bedroom and won't speak to anyone.
   a cheerful   b moody   c hardworking

My global progress

Think about what you have studied in this unit. Answer the questions below.

1 What topics did you like and why?

2 What activities did you like and why?

3 What did you find challenging and why?

4 What help do you need now?

5 What would you like to find out more about?

6 What topics and activities relate to other subjects at your school?

5 Famous people

1 Professions

1 Word study

Complete the sentences with a profession from the box.

~~composer~~   explorer   inventor   film director
scientist   artist   entrepreneur   singer

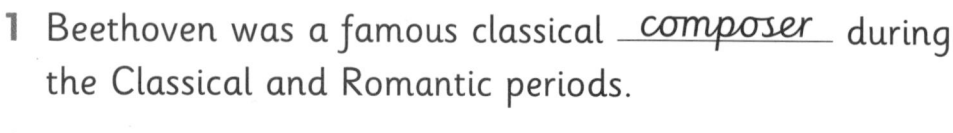

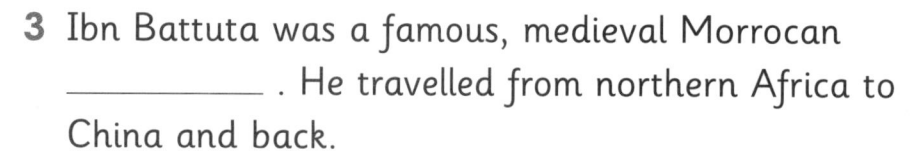

1 Beethoven was a famous classical __composer__ during the Classical and Romantic periods.

2 Louis Braille was the _____ of braille, a system of reading and writing used by people who are blind.

3 Ibn Battuta was a famous, medieval Morrocan _____ . He travelled from northern Africa to China and back.

4 Mark Zuckerberg is a famous _____ . He created the social networking website, Facebook.

5 Taylor Swift is a famous _____ from the USA.

6 Steven Spielberg is a _____ . He has directed world famous films such as *Transformers* and *Men in Black*.

7 Alexander Fleming was a famous _____ who discovered penicillin which is used to treat infections.

8 Leonardo Da Vinci was a famous _____ . His most famous work of art is the Mona Lisa.

2 Word snake

Find and circle seven adjectives in the word snake.

caringpositivedeterminedcleverfuncreativebrave

Steven Spielberg

Beethoven

Ibn Battuta

Taylor Swift

3 Vocabulary

Look at the people in the pictures and choose an adjective from Activity 2 to describe each of them. You can use words more than once.

a _____ b _____ c _____

d _____ e _____ f _____

Use of English

Modal verbs of speculation
He **could be** a scientist. She **might not be** a scientist.

0% ──────────────────────────────── 100%
can't be   might not be   might be / could be   must be

4 Use of English

Complete the sentences with the correct modal verb.

1 He's looking through a microscope. He __must__ be a scientist.

2 She's opening the backstage door of the theatre. She _____ be an actress.

3 The artist has a British accent, so he _____ be American.

4 The photographers are taking photos of her outside the concert hall. She _____ be a famous singer.

5 He's always playing the piano. He _____ be a composer.

6 She's singing at the karaoke party, so she _____ be a professional singer.

2 Famous people and their work

Strategy check! Matching headings to paragraphs
Tick the strategies which will help you match headings to paragraphs.
Use the strategies to do Activity 2.
- Look at the visual clues. ☐
- Look for key words in each paragraph. ☐
- Look at the type of text. ☐

1 **Read** the text and match headings a–d with each paragraph.

a Living in space
c Record time in space
b Being an astronaut
d The International Space Station

Have you ever dreamed of being an astronaut?

☐ The first astronauts were usually fighter pilots who could fly in difficult conditions. There were very brave, determined people who enjoyed danger. However, modern astronauts are not just jet pilots. They could be computer experts or scientists who have other useful skills for life in space.

☐ Living in space can be difficult. The biggest problem is that there is no gravity in space, so everything floats – including you! Everyday activities, such as sitting, walking and lying in bed, are impossible in space. There is no running water, so every drop on board the spaceship is precious.

☐ The International Space Station is the biggest object in space. It travels around Earth at 27 700 kilometres per hour. At night, it can be seen from Earth flying 360 kilometres above us. It was built by 16 different countries including: USA, Russia, Japan and Canada. The astronauts do lots of experiments both inside and outside the space station. Outside, the spacewalkers wear protective suits to protect them from radiation, and they are carried by a robotic arm so they don't float off!

☐ Astronauts can spend many hours in space. Sergei Krikalev has spent the most time in space with a record of 803 days, 9 hours and 39 minutes which is about 2.2 years in space!

2 Read the text again and answer the questions.

1 Do all astronauts need to be fighter pilots? _No, they don't._
2 What are astronauts like? _____
3 Which everyday activities can't you do in space? _____
4 How fast does the International Space Station travel around Earth?
_____
5 What is a robotic arm used for? _____
6 What is the astronaut Sergei Krikalev famous for?
_____

62 3 Pronunciation Large numbers
Match the words to the numbers.

1 one hundred and fifty-five thousand _b_   a 27 700
2 sixteen thousand, eight hundred and sixty-five   b 155 000
3 twelve million   c 12 000 000
4 twenty-seven thousand, seven hundred   d 188 000 000
5 one hundred and eighty-eight million   e 16 865
6 four hundred and seventy-six thousand   f 476 000

62 4 Listen and repeat the numbers from Activity 3.

5 Challenge
Read and answer the questions.

1 Would you like to travel to outer space one day? Why? Why not?
2 What surprises you about living in space?
3 What would you like to see in outer space?
4 What would you miss from Earth if you were an astronaut?

_____
_____
_____

Cambridge Global English **Stage 5** Activity Book Unit 5

3 A presentation about a famous person

Strategy check! Completing notes
Tick the strategies which will help you to complete the notes.
Use them for Activity 1.
- Read the notes you have to complete before listening. ☐
- Look up the words you don't understand. ☐
- Think about the missing information: is it a verb, a noun, an adjective ...? ☐
- Listen without reading anything first. ☐

63 **1** **Listen** and complete the notes on Nelson Mandela using words from the box.

| 1918 | ~~Nelson Mandela~~ | prison | president | respected | lawyer | believed | 1990 |

I'm going to talk about ¹ _Nelson Mandela_ .
He was one of the most ² _____ people in the world.
He was born in ³ _____, in South Africa.
He studied to be a ⁴ _____ .
He ⁵ _____ in racial equality.
The government put him in ⁶ _____ for 27 years.
He came out of prison in ⁷ _____ .
He became the first black ⁸ _____ of South Africa in 1994.
He died in December 2013.

2 **Word study** Using interesting adjectives
Match the adjectives in the box to the meanings 1–6.

Someone who ...

1 looks after others is _caring_ .
2 gives a lot to others is _____ .
3 doesn't give up is _____ .
4 does something dangerous or difficult is _____ .
5 does something special and worth mentioning is _____ .

~~caring~~
remarkable
brave
generous
determined

56 Cambridge Global English Stage 5 Activity Book Unit 5

Use of English

Question tags

We use falling intonation when we are checking information we already know.
Jackie Chan **was born in** China, **wasn't** he?
We make questions tags to check information like this:

Positive sentence:	Negative question tag:
You **are** from Dubai,	**aren't** you?
He **was** a president,	**wasn't** he?
Negative sentence:	Positive question tag:
You **don't** like cheese,	**do** you?
He **didn't** study medicine,	**did** he?

Note: the question tag repeats the auxiliary verb (or main verb **be/do**) from the sentence and changes it from positive to negative or negative to positive.

3 Listen

Complete the sentences with the correct question tag from the *Use of English* box. Then listen, check and repeat.

1 Nelson Mandela was born in 1918, _wasn't he_ ?

2 He studied to be a lawyer, _____ ?

3 He was one of the most respected people in the world, _____ ?

4 Mother Teresa dedicated her life to helping others, _____ ?

5 She was very generous with her time and love, _____ ?

4 Challenge

Write a presentation about Mother Teresa. Use the prompts below to help you and adjectives from Activity 2 to make your presentation more interesting.

Name: Mother Teresa   **Born:** 26th August 1910
Profession: nun
Character: caring, generous, positive, determined
Work: helping poor, sick and children without parents
Achievements: started Missionaries of Charity in 1950, won Nobel Prize for Peace in 1979.

4 A short biography

1 Read

Match the sentences to the correct pictures.

1 Tom was born on 17th June 1982.

2 When he was a child, he dreamed of climbing tall buildings.

3 During the summer holidays, he enjoyed climbing with his dad in the mountains.

4 When he was ten years old, he joined a climbing club, but one day he fell and broke his ankle.

5 Tom was very brave and determined, so by the age of 20 he was climbing very big mountains.

6 In 2013, he conquered Mount Everest, the highest mountain in the world.

2 Use of English
Complete the sentences with linking words from the box.

because
but
so
and

1 Tom dreamed of climbing tall buildings _because_ he wanted to be a climber.

2 He enjoyed climbing, _____ he joined a climbing club.

3 _____ he was very brave and determined, Tom was climbing very big mountains by the age of 20.

4 He joined a climbing club, _____ one day he fell and broke his ankle.

5 In 2013, he climbed Mount Everest _____ conquered the highest mountain in the world.

3 Write
Complete these sentences about yourself. Use the linking words from Activity 2.

1 What do you dream of doing when you are older?
_____

2 When did you learn to ride your bike?
_____

3 What do you like about learning English?
_____

4 When did you learn how to swim?
_____

4 Complete the chart with a more detailed list of your personal achievements. Use the ideas below to help you.

exams you've passed   prizes you've won   an achievement you are proud of

Age	Achievement

5 Challenge
Write your own short biography. Use the notes you have made in the table to help you. Use linking words to join your ideas.

Cambridge Global English Stage 5 Activity Book Unit 5

5 Extracts from *The Stowaway*

1   **Read** the extracts again from *The Stowaway* in the Learner's Book.
    Decide if the sentences are **T (true)** or **F (false)** and write **T** or **F** in the boxes.
    Correct the false sentences in your notebook.

    1 *HMS Endeavour* set sail in 1768. ☐ T
    2 None of the crew knew there was a young boy hiding on board. ☐
    3 He hid in another boat on board *Endeavour*. ☐
    4 When he looks over the edge of the boat, he gets noticed. ☐
    5 The bell on the ship clangs every hour. ☐
    6 The animals on board are noisy all day and all night. ☐
    7 He would like his father to find him and take him home. ☐
    8 Nicholas worked for the butcher. ☐
    9 He is more intelligent than his brothers. ☐
    10 He wants to show his father that he is wrong about him. ☐

2 **Vocabulary**
   Circle the adjectives you think best describe Nicholas.

   > generous   brave   caring   positive   fun   determined   foolish

3 **Write**
   What advice would you give to Nicholas? Write your suggestion.

   Nicholas should _____

4 Vocabulary

Complete the sentences with a word from the box.

> ~~anchor~~   prow   rigging   sails   ship's bell

1 The captain dropped the _anchor_ when the ship arrived in the port.
2 The wind fills the ship's _____ .
3 They hear the _____ _____ every hour.
4 The sailors pulled the _____ to tighten the sails.
5 The captain stood on the _____ of the ship, looking out to sea.

5 Match the words to their meanings.

1 dangerous   a stern
2 a student   b courageous
3 serious   c a scholar
4 brave   d worthless
5 not valuable   e perilous

6 Values Showing the best of ourselves

Circle the word that you think is a good quality in a person.

1 selfish / generous
2 dependent / independent
3 foolish / sensible
4 kind / unkind
5 caring / uncaring

Which of these qualities do you have? Give a reason why.

I'm _____ because _____
_____
_____ .

6 Unit 5 Revision

1 Vocabulary

Complete the sentences with the correct word. You can use the words more than once.

> caring singer film director skilled scientist writer entrepreneur determined

1 A _____ does a lot of experiments.
2 A _____ is good at organising actors and actresses.
3 A _____ has a good voice.
4 A _____ is imaginative.
5 An _____ has good ideas for business.
6 A nurse is a _____ person.
7 A builder is _____ .
8 An athlete is _____ .

2 Use of English

Circle the correct answer.

1 He looks after patients in a hospital. He **might be** / **must be** a doctor.
2 He always carries a video camera and he wears a baseball cap.
   He **can't be** / **might be** a film director.
3 She's always playing her piano. She **could be** / **can't be** a composer.
4 Nelson Mandela was a president, **was he** / **wasn't he**?
5 Mother Teresa won the Nobel Peace Prize, **didn't she** / **wasn't she**?
6 Captain Cook's ship was called *Endeavour*, **was it** / **wasn't it**?
7 We've nearly finished the unit, **have we** / **haven't we**?

3 Over to you

Complete these sentences with your own ideas.

1 When I'm older I want to be _____ .
2 My friend might be a _____ .
3 I think I'm a _____ person.
4 I want to be more _____ in the future.

My global progress

Think about what you have studied in this unit. Answer the questions below.

1 What topics did you like and why?

2 What activities did you like and why?

3 What did you find challenging and why?

4 What help do you need now?

5 What would you like to find out more about?

6 What topics and activities relate to other subjects at your school?

6 Myths and fables

1 Understanding myths and legends

1 **Read** and match the descriptions.

1 **The deadly serpent of Koshi** was an enormous Japanese serpent with eight heads and eight tails. Each head had two red eyes. It was so long that its body covered eight hills and eight valleys. Trees and grass often grew on its back! It tried to get into the village of Izumo, but a knight cut off the serpent's eight heads!

a

2 **The Aspidochelone was a gigantic turtle** with huge tusks that lived off the coast of India. Its shell was so big that when it was sleeping it looked like a small island. In fact, one of the first reports of seeing this beast was by Alexander the Great when he was in India. A group of his men went to explore an island looking for treasure of a dead king. The men landed on the island, but one hour later it sank into the sea. It was Aspidochelone!

b

3 **The Kraken is a legendary sea monster** which looked like a giant octopus. When it was still it looked like an island. It was as long as ten ships and as high as the top of a ship's sailing mast. When it attacked a ship, it wrapped its many tentacles around it and pulled it into the sea and the crew drowned. What is really amazing about these stories is that scientists believe these creatures may exist – somewhere!

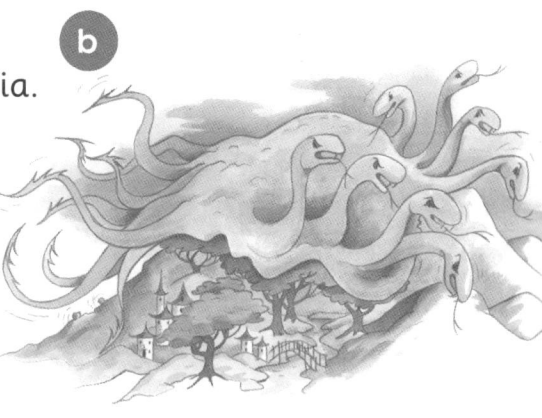

c

64   Cambridge Global English Stage 5 Activity Book Unit 6

2 Read the descriptions again and write **A** (Aspidochelone), **K** (Koshi) or **Kr** (Kraken).

1 It had tusks. _A_
2 A brave man killed it. ___
3 It was a turtle. ___
4 It attacked ships. ___
5 It was discovered by Alexander the Great. ___
6 It had eight heads. ___
7 It lived near India. ___
8 It was Japanese. ___

3 Use of English
Complete the sentences using the conjunctions in the box.

| if   but   so   ~~when~~   where   and |

Use of English

Conjunctions
Use **if**, **and**, **but**, **where**, **so** and **when** to join different parts of a sentence together.

1 Kraken looked like an island _when_ it was still.
2 The local people told the men that there was treasure on the island, _____ they decided to go and explore it.
3 The men landed on the island, _____ one hour later it sank into the sea.
4 Koshi might have hurt people _____ the knight hadn't killed it.
5 The coast off India is _____ Aspidochelone lived.
6 Koshi tried to get into the village, _____ the knight killed it.

4 Challenge
Draw your own mythical creature. Describe it and write about what it did.

2 Fables

Reading strategy Finding specific information in a text

Tick the strategies that will help you find specific information in a text. Use the strategies to read the text below.

- Think about what you want to find out before your read a text. ☐
- Scan for key words in a text. ☐
- Use your dictionary to check the meaning of the words you don't understand. ☐

1 **Read** the fable about the Ant and the Dove. Which picture doesn't represent the story?

An ant went to the river to have a drink, but the rush of the water carried him away and the ant couldn't swim. A dove sitting on a tree overhanging the water, seeing him, immediately took a branch from the tree and let it fall close to the ant, so that he could climb on it. The dove saved the ant from drowning.

A few days later, a hunter came and pointed a gun at the dove who was sitting in the same tree. The ant was nearby and saw what the hunter wanted to do, so he stung him on the foot. The pain made the hunter miss the dove and, instead, the shot scared the dove and made her fly away.

2 Answer these questions in your notebook.

1 Why did the ant go to the river?
2 How did the dove help the ant?
3 What did the hunter want to do?
4 How did the ant help the dove?

3 What is this fable about? Circle the correct answer below.

being responsible   being kind   being honest

4 Vocabulary Prefixes *un-, ir-, dis-*

Match the words with the correct prefix to make the negative.

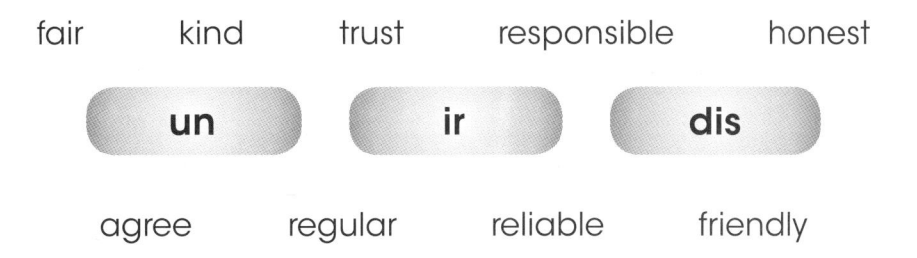

fair   kind   trust   responsible   honest

un   **ir**   **dis**

agree   regular   reliable   friendly

5 Do the questionnaire with a friend or someone in your family.
Circle their answer and write their reason.

	always	sometimes	never
1 Are you kind? He / She _____			
2 Are you responsible? _____			
3 Are you friendly? _____			
4 Are you reliable? _____			
5 Are you honest? _____			
6 Are you fair? _____			

6 **Challenge**

Write a report about the person you interviewed using the information above.

My (friend/sister) is sometimes irresponsible …

3 Telling an anecdote

1. Look at the pictures which illustrate this story. Use these prompts to summarise each picture. Use the past simple.

1 arrive / hotel. *The family arrived at the hotel.*

2 go / beach _____

3 have / dinner _____

4 go / to bed _____

5 mum / feed / baby _____

6 she / see / something _____

7 the young girl / point / something (in the corridor) _____

2 What do you think the young girl saw?

_____

_____

_____

> **Use of English**
>
> **Past simple and past continuous**
> I **was walking** in the mountains **when** I **heard** a noise.
> **As** we **were walking** we **saw** something behind a tree.

3 Use of English

Complete these sentences about the anecdote using the past simple or the past continuous form of the verb in brackets. Use the pictures to help you.

1 The girl _____ (drop) her doll as the family _____ (walk) in.

2 The wind _____ (blow) the newspaper out of mum's hands as dad _____ (swim) in the sea.

3 Mum _____ (feed) the baby when she _____ (see) a shadow in the corridor.

4 The family _____ (leave) the hotel room when the young girl _____ (see) something strange.

4 Write

Now write the anecdote using your answers from Activities 1 and 3 with the time expressions below.

| One summer's day | In the afternoon | In the evening |
| At night | During the night | The next day |

5 Challenge

Use your imagination and complete these sentences as if you were writing your own anecdote. Use the past simple or past continuous.

1 I was swimming in the sea when _____.

2 I saw a strange creature when _____.

3 I was walking in the park when _____.

4 I heard a strange noise as _____.

5 I was falling asleep when _____.

4 Lessons in life

1 **Read** these proverbs from around the world and match them with the pictures below.

1 Practice makes perfect.

2 Many hands make light work.

3 Think before you act.

4 A leopard cannot change its spots.

5 A trouble shared is a trouble halved.

2 Match the meanings to the proverbs.

1 We need to keeping trying at things if we want to be good at them.

2 A person's personality can't change.

3 If we talk about our problems to someone else it makes us feel better.

4 Think about what you are going to do before you do it.

5 If we all work together the work is easier.

70 Cambridge Global English Stage 5 Activity Book Unit 6

3 Read the story below. Then punctuate the missing sentences and use them to complete the story.

a You'll just have to stay there until you get thin again

b Where am I going to find something to eat he cried to himself

c Marvellous he said

d Tee-hee-hee

It was a cold winter day and Felix the Fox was very hungry. ¹_____
As he passed a big oak tree he could smell something delicious. Inside a hole in the trunk was some bread and meat that a man had left there. Felix crept inside, and he ate and he ate and he ate.
²_____ licking his lips when he'd finished the very last bit, but when he tried to get out of the tree, he couldn't! His tummy was so fat! He squeezed … and he squeezed … but it was no good. He was stuck.
³_____ laughed a bee buzzing past. ⁴_____
And by the time Felix got out, he was as hungry as before!

4 Read the complete story again. Which proverb from Activity 1 does it match?

5 **Challenge**

Write your own short story based on one of the proverbs in Activity 1. Before you start writing, brainstorm ideas for your story.

1 Where is the setting for the story?

2 How many characters are there?

3 What are they like?

4 What are they doing?

5 Is there a problem?

6 How is the problem solved?

7 What is the outcome/resolution?

5 The Lambton Worm

1 **Read** the poem *The Lambton Worm* again, and order the sentences.

1 He threw it in the well. ____

2 The worm ate calves, lambs and sheep ... even kids! ____

3 He caught a strange fish. ____

4 John went fishing. _1_

5 The worm grew and grew. ____

6 He came home and killed it. ____

7 When it was full, it fell asleep wrapped around Penshaw Hill. ____

8 Sir John heard news of the terrible worm. ____

2 Match the rhyming words.

size tell sheep hill

well fill eyes asleep

3 Complete the lines of the poem with the rhyming words. Then read the poem to check.

1 Young Lambton could not _tell_

So he threw it down a ____ .

2 And grew an awful ____

And great big goggly ____ .

3 On calves and lambs and ____ .

When they were fast ____ .

4 And it had had its ____ .

Ten times round Penshaw ____ .

4 Read the description of the Lambton Worm in your Learner's Book and draw a picture of it.

5 **Pronunciation** Stressed and unstressed words
Listen and mark the stressed words in the lines of the poem as shown in the first line. Practise saying the verse.

This scáry worm would often feéd

On calves and lambs and sheep.

And swallow little kids alive

When they were fast asleep.

6 **Values** Are you courageous?

1 **If you see a spider in your bedroom, do you ...**
   a jump on your bed and scream?
   b pick it up and throw it out of the window?

2 **If you go to the attraction park with friends, do you ...**
   a go on the scariest ride first?
   b go on the scary ride only because your friends want to?

3 **You are at the swimming pool with friends. Do you ...**
   a jump off the highest diving board without thinking about it?
   b sit down and look over the side before deciding to walk back down the steps?

Answers:
if you have answered mainly As then you are very courageous – nothing scares you! If you have answered mainly Bs then you are definitely frightened of a lot of things. Try to be a bit more courageous!

6 Unit 6 Revision

1 Crossword
Read the clues and complete the crossword.

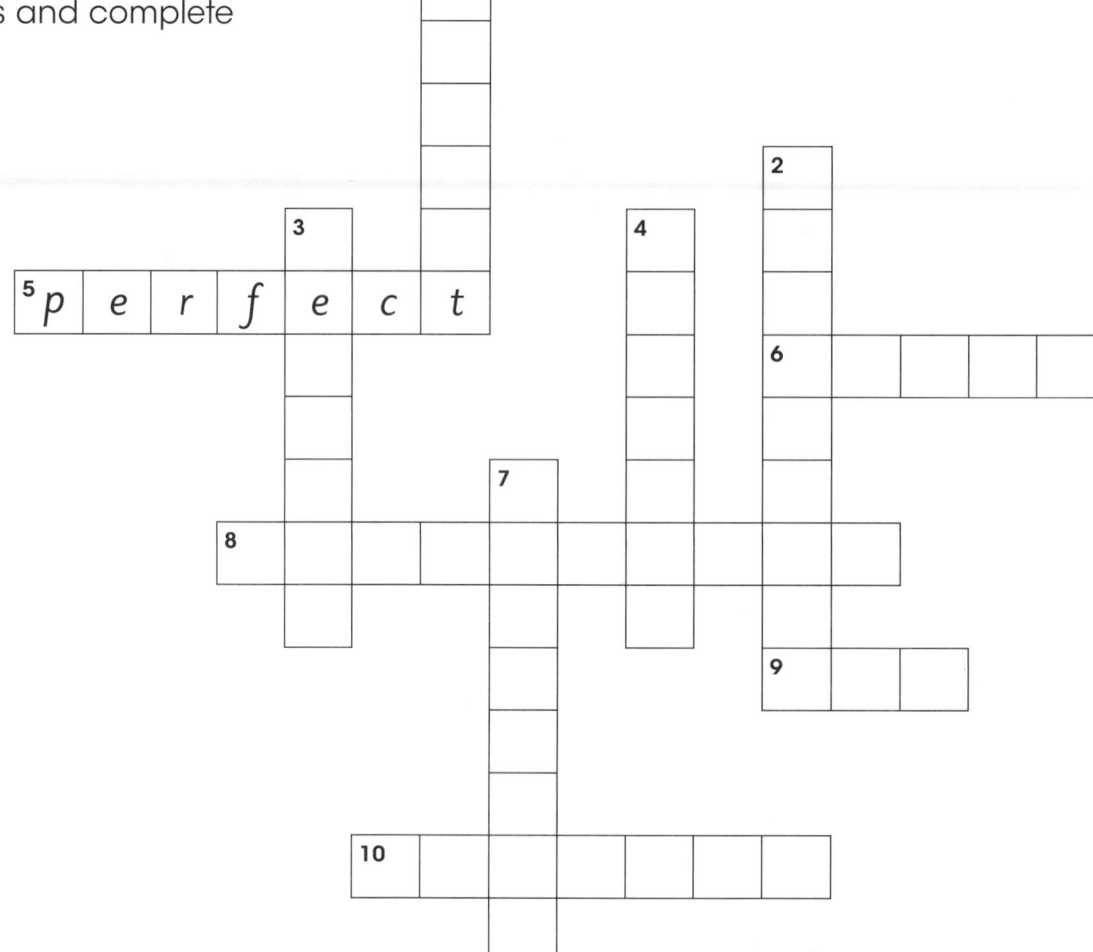

⁵p e r f e c t

Down ↓

1 Someone who always tells the truth.

2 Kraken had a lot of these.

3 I was _____ the newspaper when I heard a noise.

4 Koshi was an enormous _____ .

7 If you don't agree with someone.

Across →

5 Practice makes _perfect_ .

6 _____ before you act.

8 Someone who is not friendly.

9 The young girl _____ a ghost.

10 Mum was _____ the baby when she saw something strange.

My global progress

Think about what you have studied in this unit. Answer the questions below.

1 What topics did you like and why?

2 What activities did you like and why?

3 What did you find challenging and why?

4 What help do you need now?

5 What would you like to find out more about?

6 What topics and activities relate to other subjects at your school?

7 Ancient civilisations

1 Ancient Egypt and Rome

1 Vocabulary

Complete the sentences about ancient civilisations and then match each one to a picture.

1 The _Pyramids_ were the tombs of the Egyptian Pharaohs.

2 A _____ fought against wild animals.

3 People bathed in the Roman _____ .

4 All the organs (except the heart) of the dead Pharaoh were put in a _____ .

5 Romans watched shows in an _____ .

6 A preserved body is called a _____ .

7 An _____ transported fresh water to the Roman city.

8 The _____ guarded the tomb of the Pharaoh.

9 Romans used _____ to write numbers.

2 Read about Maya's description about the Pyramids. Complete the sentences.

The Pyramids are amazing buildings! They were built as royal tombs for the Kings in ancient Egypt. Archaeologists say that it took about 100 000 men about 20 years to build the Great Pyramid of Giza. Inside the Pyramid there were secret passageways, rooms for all the King's possessions and lots and lots of jewels and treasure. Some had trap doors too to catch robbers. I'm sure that the burial chambers were spectacular, and the beautiful paintings of the King's life must be very interesting to see. I'd love to visit the Pyramids one day.

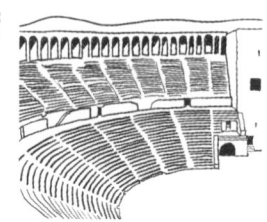

Use of English

Subordinate clauses

think, know, believe
People **believed that** this creature guarded the Pharaoh's tomb.

1 Maya thinks *that the Pyramids are amazing*_____.

2 She knows that _____.

3 Archaeologists know _____.

4 Maya believes _____.

5 She knows that _____.

3 Challenge Egyptian hieroglyphics

Look at these hieroglyphic symbols and write words in hieroglyphs for your friend to guess.

A **a**pple	B **b**aby	C **c**amel	D **d**og	E **e**at
F **f**ish	G **g**irl	H **h**at	I **i**nsect	J **j**ungle
K **k**id	L **l**ion	M **m**ummy	N **N**ile	O **o**range
P **p**en	Q **q**ueen	R **r**un	S **s**it	T **t**ime
U **u**nder	V **v**iper	W **w**indow	X **f**ix	Y **y**ellow	Z **z**ebra

Cambridge Global English **Stage 5** Activity Book Unit 7

2 Egyptian pyramids

Strategy check! Use your own knowledge
Tick the strategies that will help you use your own knowledge.
- Talk about what you know about the topic. ☐
- Look for key words in the text. ☐
- Think of questions before reading. ☐
- Think of questions you'd like to find the answer to in the text. ☐

1 Read
Look at the pictures and make a list of questions about Egyptian mummies. Then read the text and find the answers.

My questions about mummies:
_____
_____
_____

DID YOU KNOW that about 70 million mummies were made in ancient Egypt over 3000 years?

The bodies of the Pharaohs were preserved by embalming them. First, they took all the very important organs out of the body (apart from the heart). These were put in a canopic jar. Then, they had to get the moisture (the water) out of the body – they did this by covering the body in salt. Have you ever thought about why you are thirsty after salty food? The answer is simple. Salt removes water from things including bodies!

Next, they left the body to dry out for about 40 days. After this, creams were used to preserve the skin. Then they **stuffed** the mummy with sand and **spices**, and wrapped it in a material called **linen**. Finally, it was wrapped in a sheet called a **shroud** and put in a **sarcophagus**.

2 Use of English

Complete the sentences about the mummy-making process using the past simple passive. Put the sentences in the correct order.

> **Use of English**
>
> **Past simple passive**
>
> We use the past simple passive when the focus is on the past action and not **who** was doing the action.
> The Great Pyramid of Giza **was built** on the west side of the River Nile.
> When the person who did the action is important, we can add **by**.
> Large blocks of stone **were moved by** thousands of workers.

1 The body __was covered__ (cover) in salty crystals. ☐

2 It _____ (dry out) for about 40 days. ☐

3 The Pharoah's body _____ (preserve) by embalming it. [1]

4 It _____ (wrap) in a material called linen. ☐

5 Creams _____ (use) to preserve the skin. ☐

6 It _____ (put) in a sarcophagus. ☐

7 It _____ (stuff) with sand and spices. ☐

8 It _____ (wrap) in a sheet called a shroud. ☐

3 Make questions and match with the correct answer.

1 Why / salt / use?
   __Why was salt used?__

2 How long / body dry out / for?
   _____

3 What / use / preserve / skin?
   _____

4 What / mummy / put in?
   _____

5 What / mummy / stuff / with?
   _____

6 What / material / mummy / wrap / in?
   _____

a 40 days

b a sarcophagus

c to dry out the body

d linen

e sand and spices

f creams

3 Everyday life in ancient times

1 **Vocabulary**
Label the things you can see in the pictures using words from the box.

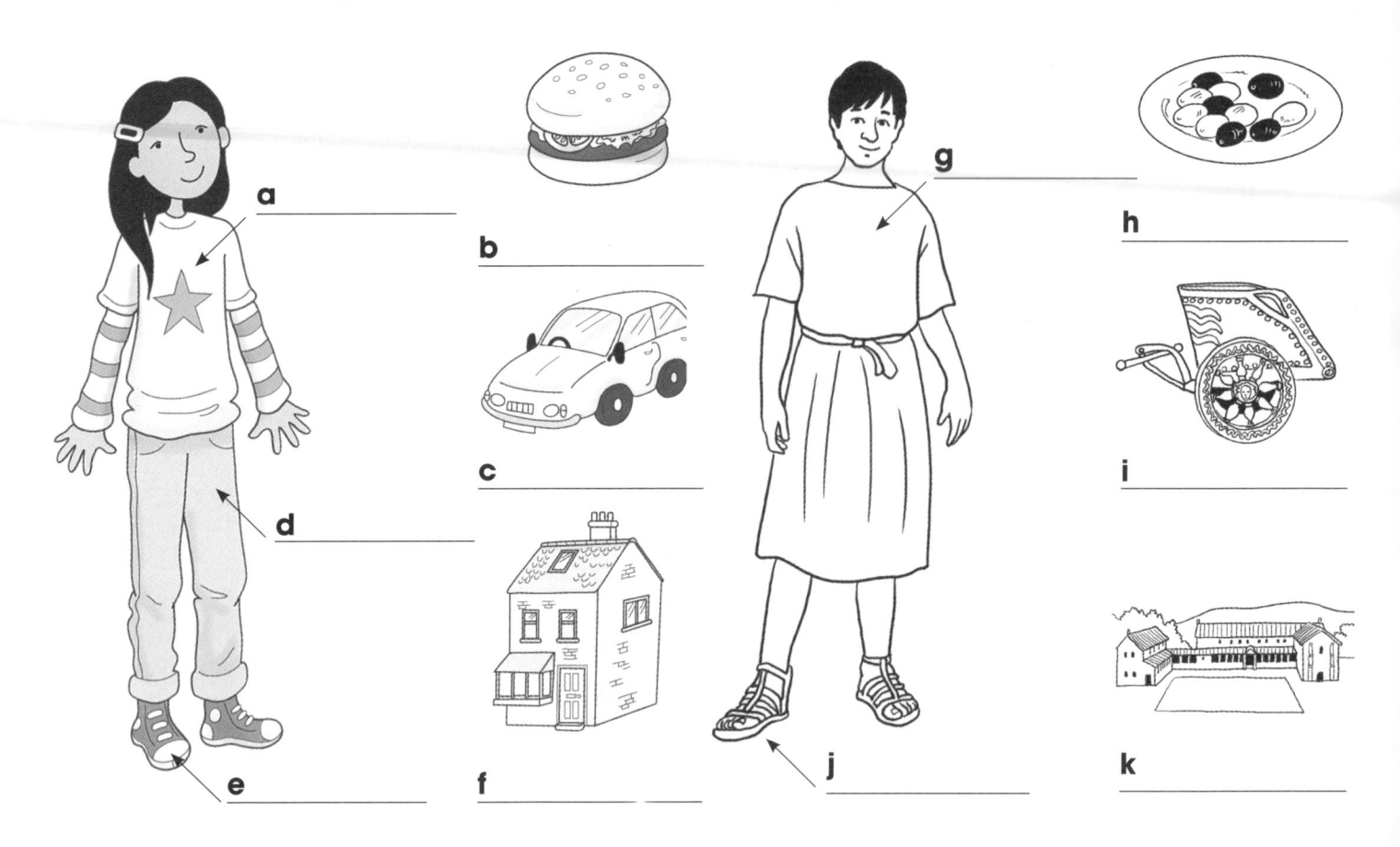

a _____
b _____
c _____
d _____
e _____
f _____
g _____
h _____
i _____
j _____
k _____

| tunic hamburger sandals baseball boots house |
| olives chariot car villa jeans t-shirt |

2 Complete the sentences using words from Activity 1.
Use **whereas**, and **too** to compare and contrast.

1 The Romans wore tunics, _whereas I wear jeans and a t-shirt_.

2 The Romans ate _____.

3 The Romans lived _____.

4 The Romans wore _____.

5 The Romans used _____.

80 Cambridge Global English Stage 5 Activity Book Unit 7

Strategy check! Listen for clues
Tick the strategies that will help you listen for clues.
- Listen for words that you already know.
- Check the meaning of words you don't understand.
- Don't try to understand every word. Be selective.

3 **Listen** to Luis talking about Roman life. Circle the topic he talks about below.

jobs   houses   entertainment   clothes   food

4 Listen again and tick the words which are the clues.

leisure time   work   kites   traditional food

dolls   apartments   togas   ball games

5 Circle the correct answer.

1 *Tali* was a game played by **boys and girls / only played by boys**.

2 The pieces were usually made from **gold and silver / animals' bones**.

3 Each piece had **six / four** sides.

4 They were thrown **at a wall / on the floor**.

5 They added up the score by calculating the numbers of the sides **facing down / facing up**.

6 Roman numerals
Look at the ways in which Roman numerals are still used today. Write the numbers.

Henry VIII

1 _____   2 _____   3 _____   4 _____

Cambridge Global English Stage 5 Activity Book Unit 7   81

4 Discoveries

1 Read the article about the discovery of some surprising Roman artefacts in London. What objects have they found? _____

DAILY NEWS

Free

Surprising discovery in London well

Yesterday, archaeologists discovered thousands of Roman artefacts at a building site in Central London. They discovered objects, such as plates and bowls, that Roman families ate their food on 2000 years ago. 'They are in excellent condition,' said the archaeologist at the site. Historians believe that London was under attack at this time from Scotland and Germany, and the Romans left London in 410 CE. 'They were found at the bottom of a deep well where they were probably put as the Romans left the city.'

They discovered some even more surprising things! An entire Roman street and the skull of a bear, which probably entertained the Romans at the nearby amphitheatre. Lots of Roman coins were found too. 'This is the best find in years!' said the archaeologist who discovered the well.

More stories inside

The well with some of the plates

2 Complete the factsheet about the discovery.

The artefacts were found ¹ _yesterday_ (When?). They were discovered by ² _____ (Who?). The site was located in ³ _____ (Where?). Many objects and places were found such as: ⁴ _____ (What?).

82 Cambridge Global English **Stage 5** Activity Book Unit 7

3 Find examples in the text of the following:

1 a quotation _____

2 a fact _____

3 an opinion _____

4 a headline _____

4 📝 Change the sentences to the past simple or past simple passive.

1 They discovered plates and bowls.

   <u>*Plates and bowls were discovered by*</u> an archaeologist.

2 The plates and bowls were found at the bottom of a well.

   Archaeologists _____ .

3 The plates and bowls were used by the Romans 2000 years ago.

   Romans _____ .

4 Archaeologists discovered the site in central London.

   The site _____ .

5 They found coins, an amphitheatre and a bear's skull too!

   _____ by the archaeologists.

5 Challenge Write

Imagine you live in the future. You have discovered a time capsule full of everyday objects you use now. Write an article about what you discover.

1 First think of and draw typical everyday items in the time capsule below.

2 Write the place and the year on the capsule.

3 Write a headline.

4 Write about the discovery — When? Where? What? Who?

5 Include facts and opinions.

6 Remember to use past tenses.

Place: _____

Year: _____

Cambridge Global English Stage 5 Activity Book Unit 7   83

5 There's a Pharaoh in Our Bath!

1 **Read** the extract from *There's a Pharaoh in Our Bath* again.
Circle **T (true)** or **F (false)**.

1 The men put the coffin on the floor before they opened it.	**T** / F
2 It was night time in the storeroom.	T / F
3 There were museum staff, mummy-cases, skeletons and stuffed rhinoceros in the storeroom with the two men.	T / F
4 The mummy-case was covered in hieroglyphics.	T / F
5 Grimstone is very patient as he waits for Professor Jelly to speak.	T / F
6 Professor Jelly wants Grimstone to stop asking him questions.	T / F
7 The mummy hasn't been in the storeroom for a long time.	T / F
8 Grimstone thinks that there is a clue to a treasure in the coffin.	T / F

2 **Vocabulary** Adjectives
Match the adjectives to the part of the face or body they describe.

> moon-like ~~pudgy~~ hawk tubby hooded winged

1 ___pudgy___ hand
2 _____ eyebrows
3 _____ frame
4 _____ face
5 _____ nose
6 _____ eyes

3 Read the description of Grimstone's face. Draw a picture of him in the box.

Grimstone had great winged eyebrows, hooded eyes and a hawk nose.

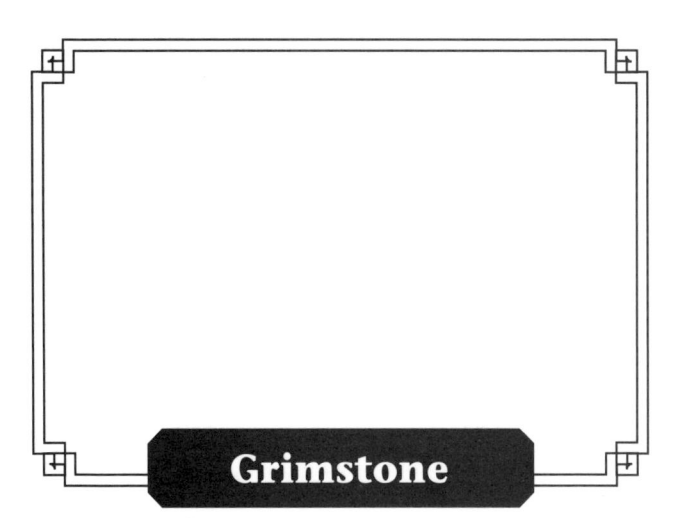

Grimstone

4 Complete the summary of the extract using the verbs in the box in the past simple passive or the past simple.

> The lid of the coffin __was pushed__ (push) back by the two men.
> They _____ (look) at the beautiful mummy case. The hieroglyphics on the case _____ (inspect) by Professor Jelly. He _____ (take) his time, so Grimstone _____ (become) _____ impatient.
> Grimstone _____ (think) there was a clue to the treasure in the coffin. Jelly _____ (finish) translating the hieroglyphs on the side of the coffin.

5 **Pronunciation** Identifying tone
Listen to the direct speech and match to an emotion.

1 'Shall I open the school report now?'   a excited
2 'Why did you do that?'   b impatient
3 'Mum, are you ready now?'   c angry
4 'Open the door, it could be him.'   d worried

6 **Values** The importance of being patient
Write sentences about situations in which you need to be patient.

1 I need to be patient __on a long journey__.
2 I need to be patient _____.
3 _____.
4 _____.

Cambridge Global English Stage 5 Activity Book Unit 7   85

6 Unit 7 Revision

1 Multiple-choice quiz
Choose the correct word to complete the sentences.

1 The burial chambers were full of _____ .
   a robber   b chariots   c jewels and treasures

2 _____ fought against wild animals in Ancient Rome.
   a soldiers   b gladiators   c merchants

3 Mummies were put in a _____ .
   a canopic jar   b a sarcophagus   c box

4 The Pharaoh's body _____ in salty crystals.
   a was stuffed   b was covered   c was wrapped

5 Creams were used to preserve the _____ .
   a salt   b skin   c hair

6 Romans wore _____ .
   a tunics and shoes   b togas and boots   c tunics and sandals

7 They travelled in chariots _____ , I travel by car.
   a whereas   b both   c so

8 The year is _____ (MMXVI).
   a 2015   b 2016   c 2014

9 The Roman artefacts _____ in a well in London.
   a was discovered   b discovered   c were discovered

10 Grimstone had a _____ nose.
   a hooded   b hawk   c pudgy

11 Professor Jelly had a _____ hand.
   a winged   b pudgy   c moon-like

12 If you are _____ , you don't mind waiting for people.
   a impatient   b excited   c patient

My global progress

Think about what you have studied in this unit. Answer the questions below.

1 What topics did you like and why?

2 What activities did you like and why?

3 What did you find challenging and why?

4 What help do you need now?

5 What would you like to find out more about?

6 What topics and activities relate to other subjects at your school?

8 Weather and climate

1 Describing the weather

1 Vocabulary

Reorder the letters in the pictures and label the types of weather.

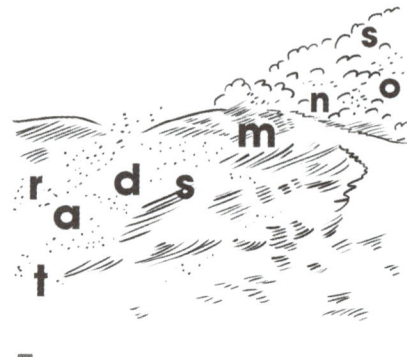

1 _flood_   2 _____   3 _____

4 _____   5 _____   6 _____

2 Weather collocations

Circle the correct answer.

1 Today there will be _____ rain, so don't forget your umbrella!

  a severe   b torrential   c high

2 _____ flooding is expected if it continues to rain.

  a High   b Violent   c Severe

3 During a typhoon there are _____ winds.

  a torrential   b strong   c heavy

4 Tornados are _____ and very destructive.

  a heavy   b violent   c torrential

88 Cambridge Global English Stage 5 Activity Book Unit 8

3 Read the text and match the questions with the correct part.

- How fast do they travel?
- ~~What is a tornado?~~
- What should you do?
- What do they look like?

TORNADOES

1 _What are tornadoes_ ?

Tornadoes (or twisters) are spiral, violent winds that can destroy everything in their path.

2 _____?

They are large, funnel-type clouds, like a long rope sweeping across the land. They can be black, grey or even white.

3 _____?

They travel at different speeds and can last from a few minutes up to an hour.

4 _____?

They are very dangerous, so you must follow this advice if there is a tornado warning:

- The safest place to be during a tornado is in a tornado shelter or a basement. If you are not near one then a bathroom with no windows is a good place.
- Protect your head and neck by pulling a bed mattress or sleeping bag over your head.
- Keep water, food and a first aid kit in the shelter and don't leave until you are sure the tornado has passed.

4 Challenge

Write about an extreme weather situation you have experienced in your country.

Describe the type of weather.

How long did it last?

What did you do?

How did you feel?

2 Rainforests

1 **Vocabulary**

Read about and label the different parts of the rainforest, and the animals that live there. Use your dictionary to check the words you don't know.

1 _____
2 _____
3 _____
4 _____
5 _____
6 _____
7 _____
8 _____
9 _____
10 _____
11 _____
12 _____
13 _____

Emergent layer: This is the tallest layer in the forest where there are giant trees. Only fliers and gliders live here, such as the **harpy eagle** and the **pygmy glider**.

Canopy: This is the upper part of the leafy trees. It is full of animal life and the noisiest part of the forest. This is where the **sloth** lives, as well as the **spider monkey** and the **toucan**.

Understory: This is a cool, dark environment under the leaves of the trees. It is home to animals like the **red-eyed tree frog** and **boa constrictor**.

Forest floor: Many insects and other bugs live here such as the large, **leafcutter ants** and **hairy caterpillars** with stinging hairs which protect them from predators.

Cambridge Global English **Stage 5 Activity Book Unit 8**

Strategy check! Giving your opinion
Tick the strategies that will help you form an opinion about a text.

- Think carefully about the information given in the text. Do you agree or disagree with it? ☐
- Evaluate the text carefully as you read. ☐
- Ask your teacher for the answer. ☐

2 Read

What has your furniture, your toys and the food you eat have in common? Do you know? If not then read on to find out.

Rainforests and our daily life

Medicines
A lot of the medicines we use are made from plants which grow in the rainforests. Medicines that can help cure skin diseases and heart disease are just some of the hundreds of medicines made from rainforest plants.

Even if you live in a large city far away from the tropical rainforests, you need a healthy rainforest for your everyday needs.

Food
There are many types of food and drinks in our diet that come from the rainforests. Not surprisingly, lots of fruits, such as bananas, kiwis, mangos, pineapples and papayas, grow there because of the hot, humid climate. Coffee beans and tea also grow in these areas. Have you ever thought about where the sugar you put in your drinks comes from, or the cocoa in your hot chocolate or milkshake? Yes, the rainforests!

Wood
Just look at all the things that are made of wood: tables, chairs, toys. Well, a lot of this wood comes from the rainforests too.

So, if you think the rainforests are too far away for you to care about, remember that a healthy rainforest is important for us all, and the future of our beautiful planet, Earth.

3 Give your opinion about the information you have discovered in the text.

Write a sentence about:

- something you have found out. _____
- something that has surprised you. _____
- something that you think is very important. _____

3 Extreme weather

1 Read the online weather report for Brazil tomorrow. Draw the weather symbols on the map and write the temperature.

Manaus Temp °C _____

Porto Velho Temp °C _____

Recife Temp °C _____

Porto Alegre Temp °C _____

Tomorrow morning, in the north of Brazil, it will be sunny and a little cloudy. Manaus will have a high of 20 degrees. It will be very humid in the rainforests and there is possibility of a thunderstorm later on in the afternoon. In Recife, on the east coast, it will be cloudy with some light rain, and a high of 21 degrees. In the south, in Porto Alegre, it will be bright and sunny, with a high of 26 degrees, and in the west, in Porto Velho, it will be very humid and stormy with a high of 25 degrees. The weather for the rest of the week will be the same.

2 Read Habib's blog about his trip along the Amazon River in Brazil. How accurate was the weather report in Activity 1? Circle the differences in his blog below.

my blog friends photos links

Today I began my trip along the Amazon River. I left Manaus early in the morning on a beautiful Amazon river boat. It was a bright sunny day and the temperature was 25 degrees. After a delicious lunch on board, we did some fishing. Not for long though because there was a thunderstorm, and we all had to go inside the boat.

Cambridge Global English **Stage 5** Activity Book Unit 8

3 Look at the weather and temperatures. Circle the correct words.

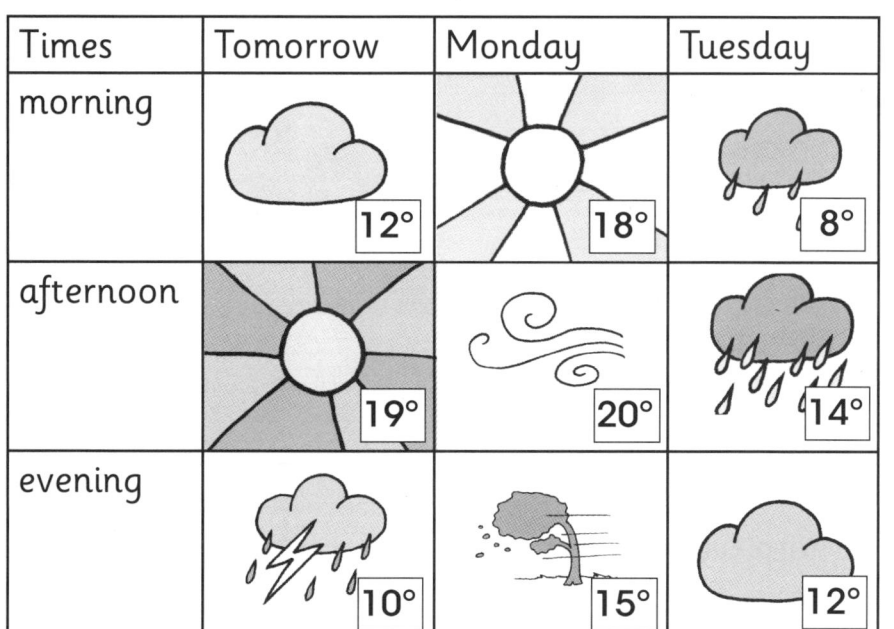

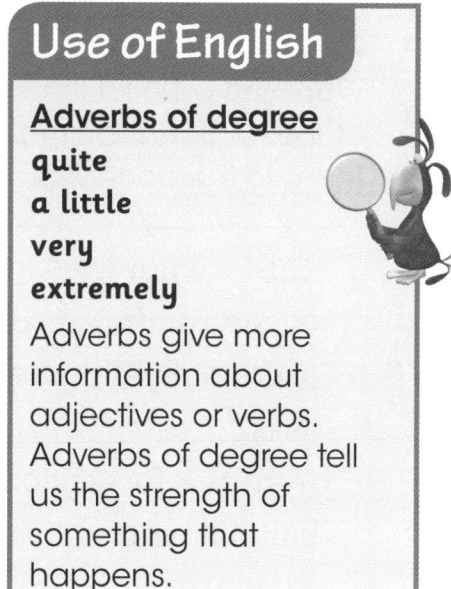

Times	Tomorrow	Monday	Tuesday
morning	cloudy 12°	sunny 18°	rainy 8°
afternoon	sunny 19°	windy 20°	rainy 14°
evening	stormy 10°	windy 15°	cloudy 12°

Use of English

Adverbs of degree
quite
a little
very
extremely
Adverbs give more information about adjectives or verbs. Adverbs of degree tell us the strength of something that happens.

1 Tomorrow morning, it will be cloudy and (quite) / extremely cold so don't forget your coat.

2 Tomorrow evening, it will be **very stormy** / **quite cloudy**, so it's best to stay indoors.

3 On Monday morning, it will be **quite windy** / **very sunny**, so don't forget your sunglasses.

4 On Monday evening, it will be **quite windy** / **extremely windy**, so be careful if you are out walking.

5 On Tuesday morning, it will be very **wet** / **hot** outside, so don't forget your umbrella.

6 On Tuesday evening, it will be **very hot and sunny** / **cloudy and quite cold**, so it's best to eat indoors.

4 Pronunciation Stressing important information
Listen and underline the stressed words. Then practise with your partner.

Tomorrow there will be <u>very</u> high winds, so be extremely careful if you are driving or out walking.

5 Challenge

Write a weather report for your town or city for tomorrow. Present it to your class. Remember to stress the important information.

4 Rainforest animals

1 Read

What am I? Read the descriptions of the rainforest animals and match them to the correct picture.

a harpy eagle
b boa constrictor 
c pygymy glider 
d toucan 

1. This animal lives in the canopy of the rainforest. It's mainly a fruit-eater, although it sometimes likes to catch a lizard or snake from the forest floor. It's got a big yellow and brown sharp bill (similar to a beak), which it uses to pick and throw fruit.

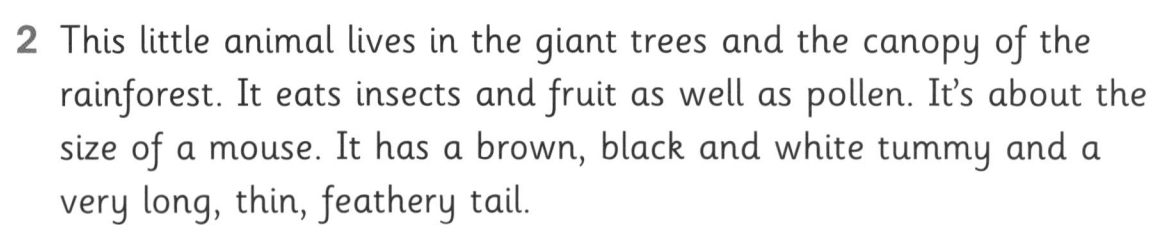

2. This little animal lives in the giant trees and the canopy of the rainforest. It eats insects and fruit as well as pollen. It's about the size of a mouse. It has a brown, black and white tummy and a very long, thin, feathery tail.

3. This long animal lives in the understory of the rainforest. It's a great hunter and likes to surprise its prey! It eats birds, frogs, lizards and rodents. It's very strong and it has circular and oval-shaped brown patterns on its body.

4. This animal lives in the emergent trees of the rainforest. It has a pale, grey head, black outer feathers and white underfeathers. It likes to eat monkeys and sloths.

2 Read the sentences and circle **T (true)** or **F (false)**.

1. A toucan eats fruit, lizards and snakes. T / F
2. A pygmy glider is bigger than a mouse. T / F
3. A pygmy glider lives in the emergent layer. T / F
4. A boa constrictor is an extremely good hunter. T / F
5. A harpy eagle has got white outer feathers and black underfeathers. T / F

Use of English

Adjective order

When we use more than one adjective to describe a noun the adjectives need to be in the following order:

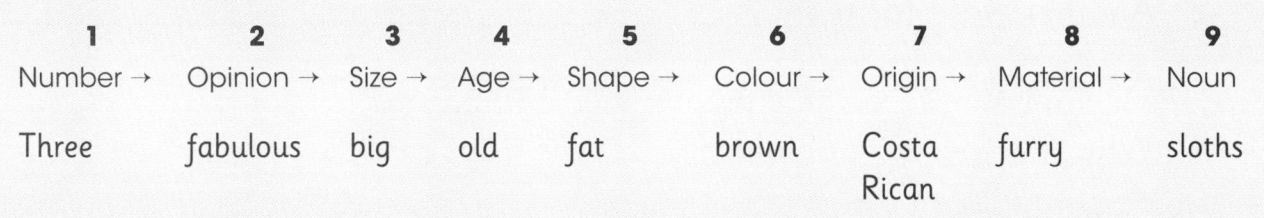

1	2	3	4	5	6	7	8	9
Number →	Opinion →	Size →	Age →	Shape →	Colour →	Origin →	Material →	Noun
Three	fabulous	big	old	fat	brown	Costa Rican	furry	sloths

3 Use of English

Reorder the adjectives to make descriptions about the animals from the text.

1 amazing / long / thin / An / tail / feathery
   <u>An amazing long, thin, feathery tail.</u>

2 tree frog / Brazilian / A / green / small

3 African / large / beautiful / grey / parrot / A

4 frightening / brown / Two / crocodiles / long-bodied / Australian

5 Three / orang-utans / enormous / long-haired

4 Challenge

Write a description about the animal in the picture. Use the information in the box to help you.

a jaguar

Location: rainforests of Central and South America

Appearance: light brown or orange, with black spots, sharp claws and teeth

Diet: fish, turtles, deer, tapirs

Behaviour: loves water, a good swimmer, sometimes climb trees

5 A visit with Mr Tree Frog and If I were a Sloth

1 Read the poem *A visit with Mr Tree Frog* again and find the following:

1. An adjective which describes his size. _tiny_ (stanza 1)
2. Another word for friend. _____ (stanza 1)
3. A noise he makes. _____ (stanza 2)
4. What his toes do at night. _____ (stanza 3)
5. Something he likes to eat. _____ (stanza 4)
6. Something he likes to eat on special occasions. _____ (stanza 4)
7. Something he's famous for. _____ (stanza 6)
8. Something his eyes do. _____ (stanza 7)
9. Something he likes to do during the day. _____ (stanza 7)
10. A superlative adjective. _____ (stanza 8)

2 Read the sentences and circle **T (true)** or **F (false)**. Correct the false sentences in your notebook.

1. Mr Tree Frog is very green. (T)/ F
2. He likes danger and often fights. T / F
3. His slime can make you better. T / F
4. He closes his eyes when he is resting. T / F
5. He likes to play during the day. T / F

3 Pronunciation
Match the rhyming words. Then listen and check.

grass   name   class
plane
fight   seen   naps   treat
street   green
night   snaps

4 Read *If I were a Sloth* again, and circle the correct answer.

1 The sloth **sits in the trees** / **hangs upside down**.
2 The sloth sleeps all day **in the understory** / **in the canopy** of the rainforest.
3 It plays when the sun **comes up** / **goes down**.
4 It eats **at night** / **during the day**.
5 It **doesn't like the noise of birds** / **makes a similar noise to a bird**.
6 It is a **common** / **an endangered** animal in the rainforest.
7 It has **long** / **extremely long** arms.
8 People will **look at me in interest** / **not see me**.

5 Action verbs
Make sentences about the sloth using these words.

~~hang~~ move play whistle nap

1 A sloth _hangs_ upside down in the trees.
2 _____
3 _____
4 _____
5 _____

6 Vocabulary Similes
Write similes about the pictures.

1 The frog is _green like the grass_.
2 She's busy _____.
3 He eats _____.

6 Unit 8 Revision

1 Vocabulary
Complete the sentences with a word from the box.

| floods | heavy | tornado | high | violent | blizzard | drought |

1 After _____ rain there are often floods.
2 A _____ is a spiral wind that travels very fast over land and sea.
3 During a typhoon there are _____ winds and _____ rain.
4 A _____ is a snowstorm.
5 After months of _____ temperatures and no rain, there was a _____ .

2 Use of English
Circle the correct answer.

If you are planning to visit a rainforest, then be prepared for ¹**quite / very** hot weather. The rainforests are very near the equator and are ²**extremely / a little** wet and humid too.

When you take a trip into the forest, you will see many of the wonderful animals and insects that live there. You might see the toucan with its ³**big, sharp / sharp, big** bill, or the harpy eagle with its ⁴**grey, pale, feathery / pale, grey, feathery** head. The ⁵**brown, old, fat / old, fat, brown** sloth could be hugging a tree and, if you listen carefully, you might hear the rattle of the ⁶**green, tiny / tiny, green** red-eyed tree frog.

3 Over to you
Write about what the weather is like today where you live. Use adverbs of degree.

| quite   a little   very   extremely |

Today the weather is _____
_____
_____
_____

My global progress

Think about what you have studied in this unit. Answer the questions below.

1 What topics did you like and why?

2 What activities did you like and why?

3 What did you find challenging and why?

4 What help do you need now?

5 What would you like to find out more about?

6 What topics and activities relate to other subjects at your school?

Cambridge Global English **Stage 5 Activity Book Unit 8**

9 Planet Earth

1 Food chains

1 **Vocabulary**

Look at the picture. Write **herbivore**, **carnivore** or **omnivore**.

a _____ b _____ c _____ d _____

e _____ f _____ g _____

2 Look at the picture and again and match the words.

1 plant   a tertiary consumer
2 a mouse   b secondary consumer
3 an owl   c producer
4 a fox   d primary consumer

3 Draw a food chain in your notebook using the animals from the picture in Activity 1. Use the example in Activity 6 on page 127 of the Learner's Book to help you.

Strategy check! Interpreting diagrams
Tick the strategies that will help you to interpret diagrams.
- Use your previous knowledge to help you.
- Use reading texts to help you understand the diagrams.
- Guess what you think the diagram means.

☐
☐
☐

4 Read the text. Label the ocean food chain with the words in bold from the text.

The ocean food chain

Let's find out what eats what in the ocean! As with any food chain, the Marine Food Chain begins with plants, such as plankton, a powerful food full of vitamins, proteins and minerals. They are **producers** because they make their own food using energy from the sun. The next link are small floating animals, such as jellyfish and starfish which eat the plankton; they are called **primary consumers**. The third link in the chain are small fish that are very common in the ocean such as minnows, which eat the small floating animals. They are called **secondary consumers**. Finally, the **tertiary consumers** are the large fish, such as tuna or small sharks, which eat the smaller ones. It's a fish-eat-fish world!

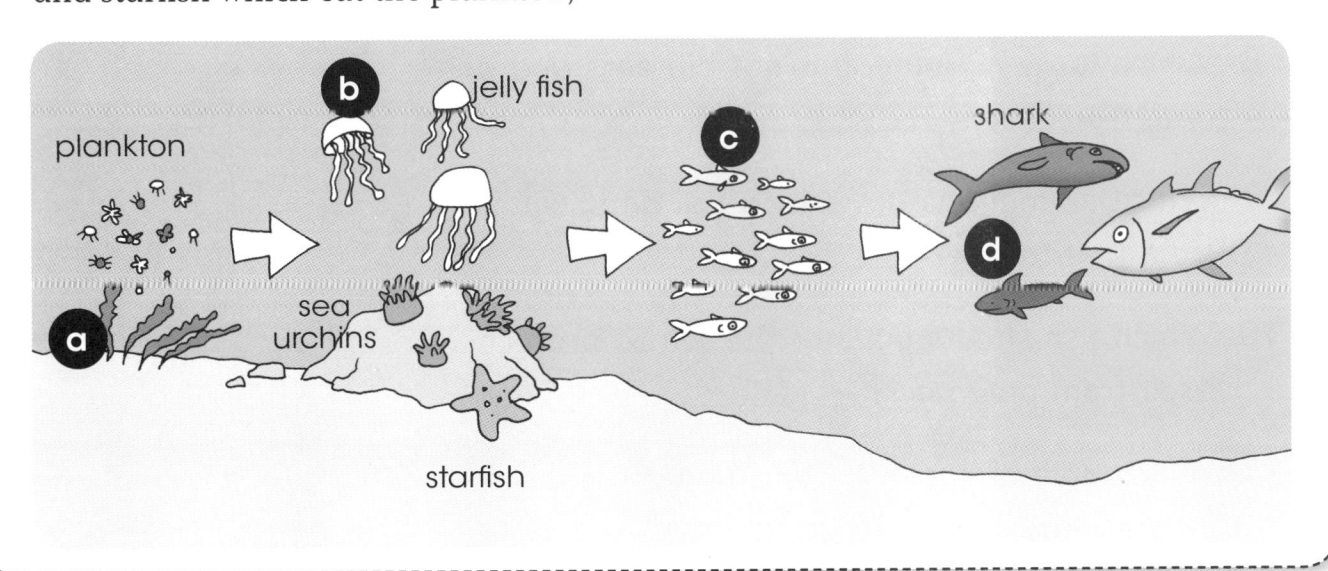

a _____ b _____ c _____ d _____

5 **Challenge**

Draw a food chain in your notebook for one of these habitats.

| forest Antarctic savannah mountain freshwater ocean desert |

2 Animal camouflage

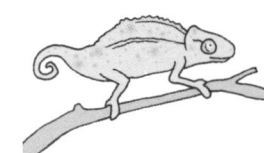

1 Do the animal quiz.

1 Which animal has got black and white stripes? _____

2 Which reptile changes its colour? _____

3 Which animal has got two big ears, a furry coat and lives in the forest? _____

4 Which animal has got two humps? _____

5 Which fish is very colourful and lives in the Indian and Pacific Oceans? _____

6 Which bird can't fly and lives in a cold climate? _____

7 Which amphibian is very tiny and lives in African rivers? _____

8 Which large mammal has got big ears and a long trunk? _____

9 Which animal has got a long tail and swings from tree to tree? _____

10 Which fish shoots ink into the sea to protect itself from predators? _____

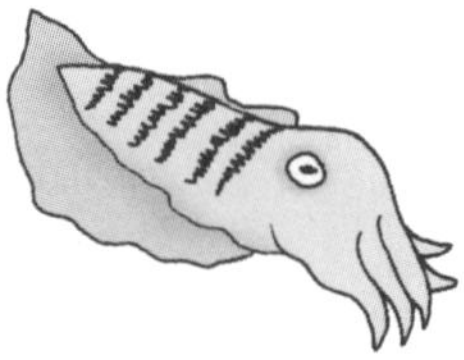

11 Which animal has got scales and a long body? _____

12 Which medium-sized mammal lives in the savannah and eats grass? _____

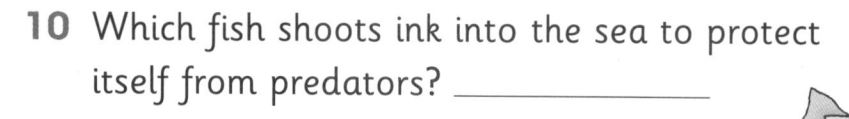

2 **Read** the short texts. Write the questions.

1 _____ The ostrich is the largest bird in the world. It lives in the African savannah and desert land. It uses its long legs to run fast in its habitat. They are so powerful that they can kill a human, or predator such as a lion.

2 _____ The zebra moves in herds of 10 to 15. Its black and white stripes camouflage it from its predators.

3 _____ The giraffe has a very long neck, so it can reach the high leaves on the trees during a drought.

4 _____ The elephant lives in hot climates, so it uses its large ears to cool itself down.

3 **Use of English**
Complete the sentences with **it** or **its**.

1 _It_ has got black and white stripes. _____ stripes protect _____ from predators.

2 _____ uses _____ powerful legs to kick predators.

3 _____ long neck helps _____ to reach the high leaves on the trees.

4 _____ flaps _____ large ears to help _____ cool down.

5 _____ uses _____ horns to protect itself from predators.

Use of English

Personal pronoun it / possessive pronoun its

We use personal pronouns instead of the name of the person, place, object or animal so that we don't repeat the name of the noun. Look at this example.
It shoots ink into the sea.
We use the possessive pronoun **its** to indicate that something belongs to a person, an animal or a place. Look at this example.
The monkey uses **its** tail to swing from tree to tree.

4 **Challenge**

Make sentences about animals using the personal pronoun **it** and the possessive pronoun **its**. Use the prompts to help you.

1 Cuttlefish: ink / protect from predators.
   Its ink protects it from predators.

2 Camel: two humps / store fat / give energy

3 Chameleon: change skin colour / protect from predators

Cambridge Global English **Stage 5 Activity Book** Unit 9

3 Looking after pets

70 **1** **Listen** to Paolo talking about his pet hamster. Put the pictures in order.

70 **2** Complete the sentences with the correct form of the words in the box. Then listen again and check.

> groom   feed   clean   exercise   look after

1 Paolo ___feeds___ his hamster twice a day.

2 Cheeks _____ on a wheel and a ladder in his cage.

3 Paolo _____ out Cheek's cage once a week.

4 Cheek _____ himself regularly by licking his fur.

5 Paolo _____ Cheek's teeth by giving him a dog biscuit to chew on.

3 Write sentences giving advice about looking after a hamster.

1 It's best to _____.

2 It's a good idea to _____.

3 It's important that _____.

104   Cambridge Global English **Stage 5** Activity Book Unit 9

Use of English

To talk about obligation and necessity we can use **must**, **should** (modal verbs) and other verbs such as **have (to)** and **need (to)**.

You **must** give your horse food every day. It's very important that …
You **should** clean it when it is dirty. It's a good idea to …
You **have to** give your horse fresh water every day. It's important to …
You **need to** look after their teeth. It's best to …
Remember to add **to** after **need** and **have**.

4 Use of English

Read the online information about having a parrot as a pet, and complete the sentences with a word from the *Use of English* box.

---

search

If you're thinking about having a parrot for a pet then read this information carefully before buying one.

First of all, **it's important** to buy a cage which is big enough for the parrot to move around in.
It's a good idea to buy toys for it to play with and **it's very important** that it has plenty of food, such as fruit, vegetables and nuts, every day. Don't forget that it needs fresh water too!

It's a good idea to wash your parrot once a week and **it's best to** visit the vet to cut their claws when they are long.

---

1 You _____ to buy a cage big enough for the parrot to move around in.

2 You _____ buy it toys to play with.

3 You _____ feed it every day.

4 You _____ wash it once a week.

5 You _____ visit the vet when it needs its claws cutting.

5 Challenge

Write your own blog about looking after a pet in your notebook.
Draw a picture of it and write advice about how to look after it.

4 Writing a leaflet

1 Complete the dialogue below with information from the leaflet.

The WILD ANIMAL Sanctuary

Species: emus, bears, African lions, tigers, foxes, raccoons, lynx ... and more!

Days: Sunday to Saturday (Mondays closed)

Opening times: 9am–8pm

Price: Adults: $10 Adults over 65 years: $7.50 Children (3 to 12 years): $7 Children under 2 years: free admission

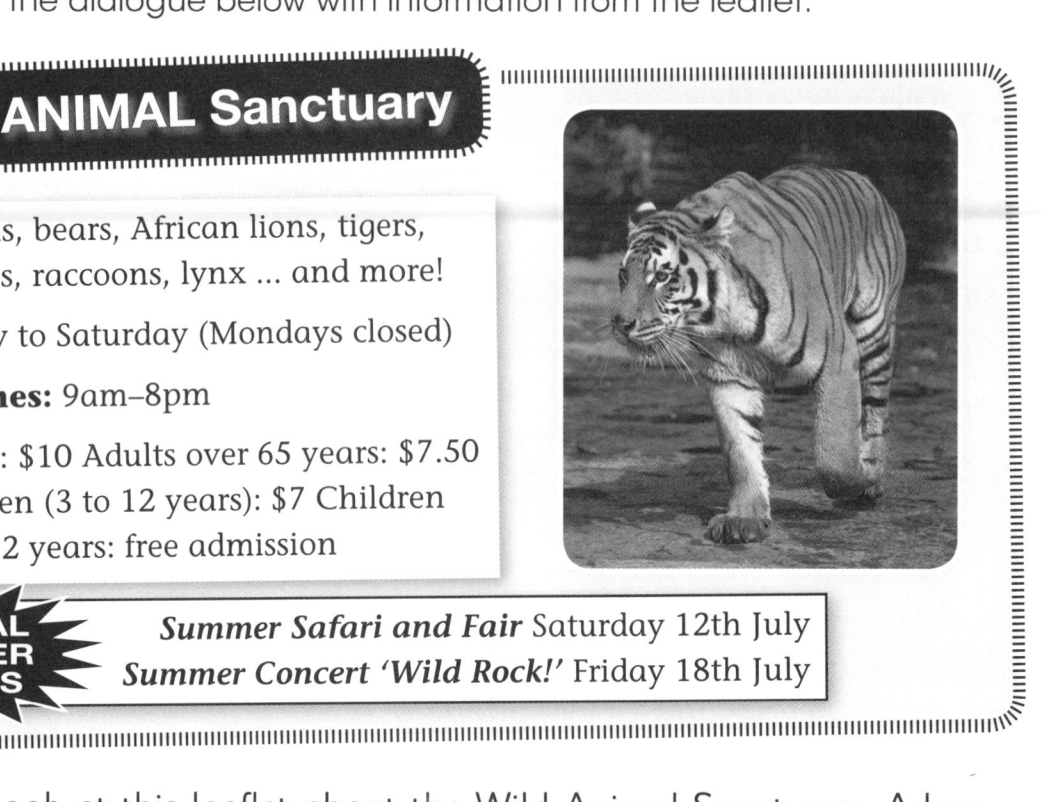

SPECIAL SUMMER EVENTS
Summer Safari and Fair Saturday 12th July
Summer Concert 'Wild Rock!' Friday 18th July

Mum: Look at this leaflet about the Wild Animal Sanctuary, Adam. Do you want to go there in the school holidays?

Adam: Yes, please – what can you see there?

Mum: There are lots of amazing animals to see! There are emus, bears and wild cats too like ¹_____, ²_____, ³_____ .

Adam: OK, that sounds great! What days is it open?

Mum: Hmmm ... . It ⁴_____ .

Adam: ... and what time does it open?

Mum: ⁵_____ .

Adam: Right, so we can spend all day there! How much will two tickets cost?

Mum: ⁶_____ .

Adam: Are there any special activities on?

Mum: Yes, there's a Summer Safari and Fair and a ⁷_____ .

Adam: I love concerts! Let's go on ⁸_____ to visit the sanctuary.

106 Cambridge Global English Stage 5 Activity Book Unit 9

2 **Problem solving**

Work out how much it will cost these families to visit the Wild Animal Sanctuary.

1 Ticket cost: $ _____

2 Tickets cost: $ _____

3 Tickets cost $ _____

3 **Write** slogans for the Wild Animal Sanctuary. Use imperative sentences.

Be the first ...   Don't miss ...   Don't leave ...   Come and ...

1 _____

2 _____

3 _____

4 _____

4 **Challenge**

The Wild Animal Sanctuary want to add another special activity to their summer plan. Imagine the activity, and write about it. Draw a picture and write a slogan for it too.

5 Mum Won't Let Me Keep a Rabbit

1 **Read** the poem again and label the pictures with the correct names.

1 ____bat____   2 _____   3 _____

4 _____   5 _____   6 _____

7 _____   8 _____   9 _____

2 **Vocabulary**
Find and circle the animals that he can't keep.

rabbitporcupinepigeonantwombatmambaelephantkangarooearwigwildebeest

3 **Pronunciation**
Complete the sentences with a rhyming word from the poem.

1 The _____ flew over the **cat**.
2 The **whale** said, 'Hello' to the _____ .
3 The **duck** was in _____ .
4 There was a _____ in the **tree**.
5 The _____ had a **feast**.

flea
bat
luck
wildebeest
snail

4 Circle the odd one out in each category and add a correct one of your own.

1 mammal   porcupine   water-rat   (ant)   _____
2 insects   flea   duck   bumblebee   _____
3 birds   pigeon   mallard   duck   toad   _____
4 amphibians   frog   toad   snake   _____
5 reptiles   lizard   rattlesnake   octopus   _____

108 Cambridge Global English Stage 5 Activity Book Unit 9

5 Reorder the words to make animal alliteration sentences and match to the correct picture.

a   b   c   d

1 lazy / log / leopard / the / lies / Larry / the / lazily / on

   _____ .

2 Betty / busy / the / buzzes / busily / bumblebee

   _____ .

3 flies / Felicity / flea / the / fat / fabulously

   _____ .

4 slowly / slimy / Sid / slides / the / snail

   _____ .

6 Choose your favourite animal from the poem. Draw a picture of it. Find out and complete the information below.

My favourite animal is:

_____

Type of animal: _____

Diet: _____

Habitat: _____

Characteristics: _____

_____

Behaviour: _____

7 **Values** Taking care of animals

Write a list of things in your notebook you have learnt about caring for animals.

You must feed them regularly.

Cambridge Global English **Stage 5 Activity Book Unit 9**

6 Unit 9 Revision

1 Crossword
Read the clues and complete the crossword.

²a n t

Down ↓

1 It flies at night and rhymes with rat.
4 A zebra has got black and white ones.
6 You need to _____ the cage once a week.
8 A _____ consumer is usually a bigger animal which eats a smaller one.
9 Camels have got two.

Across →

2 The insect the poet keeps in his garden.
3 You _____ feed your pet every day.
5 You should _____ your horse with a special brush.
7 The animal the poet keeps in his attic.
10 A _____ makes its own food.

110 Cambridge Global English Stage 5 Activity Book Unit 9

My global progress

Think about what you have studied in this unit. Answer the questions below.

1 What topics did you like and why?
   _____
   _____

2 What activities did you like and why?
   _____
   _____

3 What did you find challenging and why?
   _____
   _____

4 What help do you need now?
   _____
   _____

5 What would you like to find out more about?
   _____
   _____

6 What topics and activities relate to other subjects at your school?
   _____
   _____

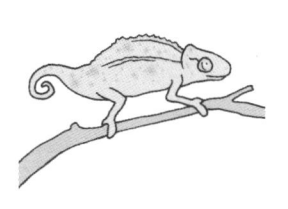

Acknowledgements

Series Editor: Kathryn Harper
Development Editor: Emma Szlachta

Cover artwork: Bill Bolton

The authors and publishers acknowledge the following sources of copyright material and are grateful for the permissions granted. While every effort has been made, it has not always been possible to identify the sources of all the material used, or to trace all copyright holders. If any omissions are brought to our notice, we will be happy to include the appropriate acknowledgements on reprinting.

Photographs
p.6 *t* Medioimages / Photodisc / Thinkstock, *c* Thomas Cockrem / Alamy, *b* Jani Bryson / iStock / Thinkstock; p.8 *t* Catherine Yeulet / iStock / Thinkstock, *b* Brand X Pictures / Stockbyte / Thinkstock; p.10 Action Plus Sports Images / Alamy; p.23 monkeybusinessimages / iStock / Thinkstock; p.29 Alex Slobodkin / iStock / Thinkstock; p.33 Getty Image / Photos.com / Thinkstock; p.41 ryabuhina / Shutterstock; p.42 *l* Ovidiu Iordachi / Hemera / Thinkstock, *r* m.bonotto / Shutterstock; p.44 Stockbyte / Thinkstock; p.46 *l* Kitch Bain / Shutterstock, *c* Akhararat Wathanasing / iStock / Thinkstock, *r* TongRo Images / Thinkstock; p.52 *t-b* AF archive / Alamy, GL Archive / Alamy, Classic Image / Alamy, AlamyCelebrity / Alamy; p.56 Mark Yeoman / Alamy; p.57 ZUMA Press, Inc. / Alamy; p.78 Jose Ignacio Soto / Shutterstock; p.81 *l* Georgios Kollidas / iStockphoto / Thinkstock, *r* Ken Durden / Shutterstock; p.89 stockbyte / Thinkstock; p.94 a Evan Bowen-Jones / Alamy, b tbkmedia.de / Alamy, c Pongphan Ruengchai / Alamy, d ktsimge / Thinkstock; p.95 stephenmeese / iStock / Thinkstock; p.105 Eric IsselTe / iStock / Thinkstock; p.106 Paul Wolf / Thinkstock

t = top
c = centre
b = bottom
l = left
r = right

Development of this publication has made use of the Cambridge English Corpus (CEC). The CEC is a multi-billion word computer database of contemporary spoken and written English. It includes British English, American English and other varieties of English. It also includes the Cambridge Learner Corpus, developed in collaboration with Cambridge English Language Assessment. Cambridge University Press has built up the CEC to provide evidence about language use that helps to produce better language teaching materials.

This product is informed by the English Vocabulary Profile, built as part of English Profile, a collaborative programme designed to enhance the learning, teaching and assessment of English worldwide. Its main funding partners are Cambridge University Press and Cambridge English Language Assessment and its aim is to create a 'profile' for English linked to the Common European Framework of Reference for Languages (CEFR). English Profile outcomes, such as the English Vocabulary Profile, will provide detailed information about the language that learners can be expected to demonstrate at each CEFR level, offering a clear benchmark for learners' proficiency. For more information, please visit www.englishprofile.org